Barbara Hepworth
Sculpture Garden

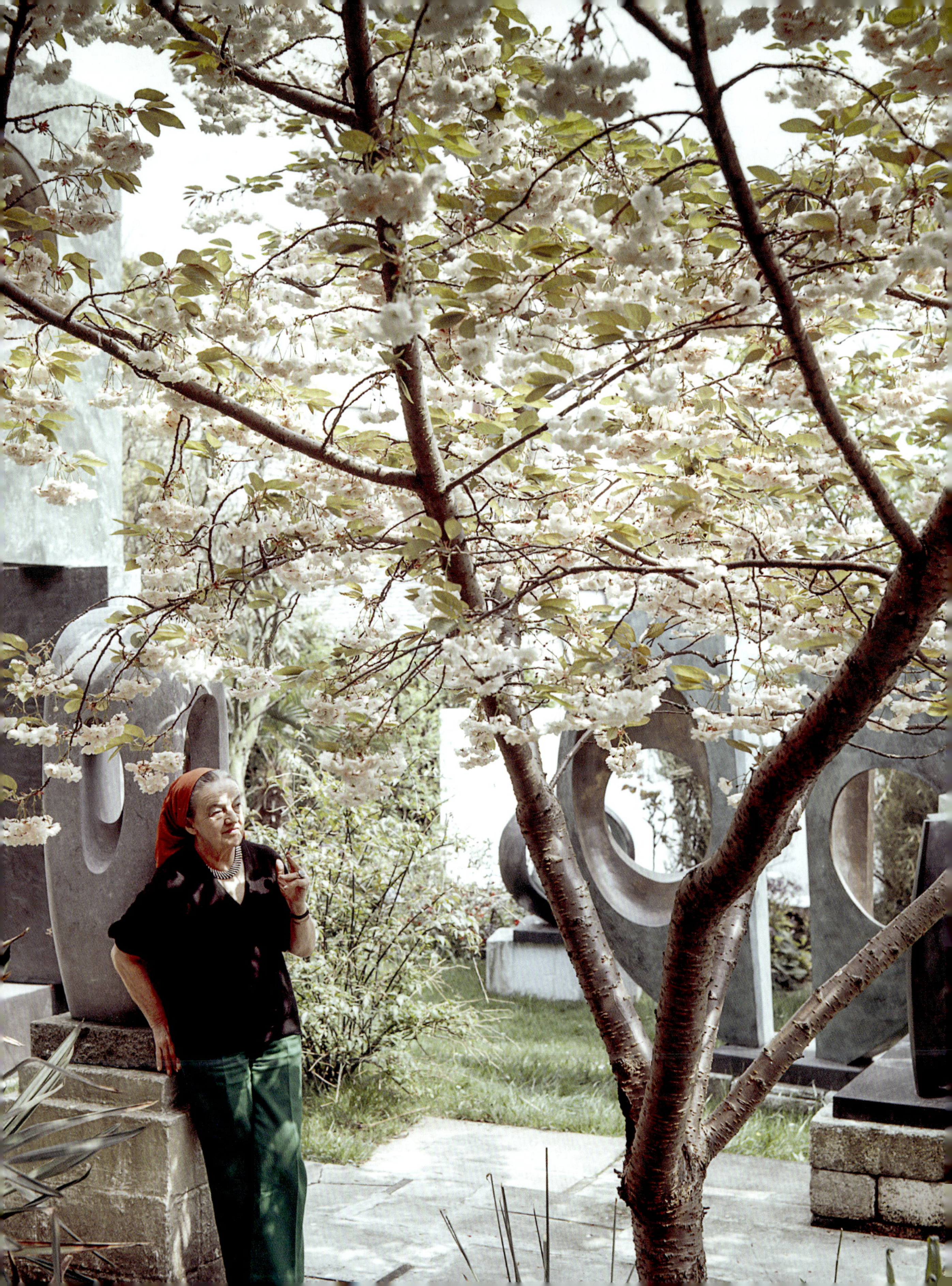

Barbara Hepworth
Sculpture Garden

Chris Stephens, Miranda Phillips
and Jodi Dickinson

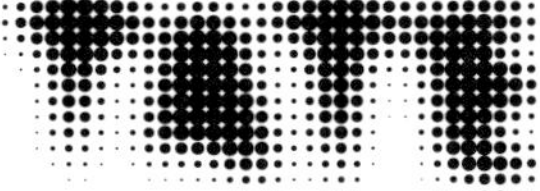

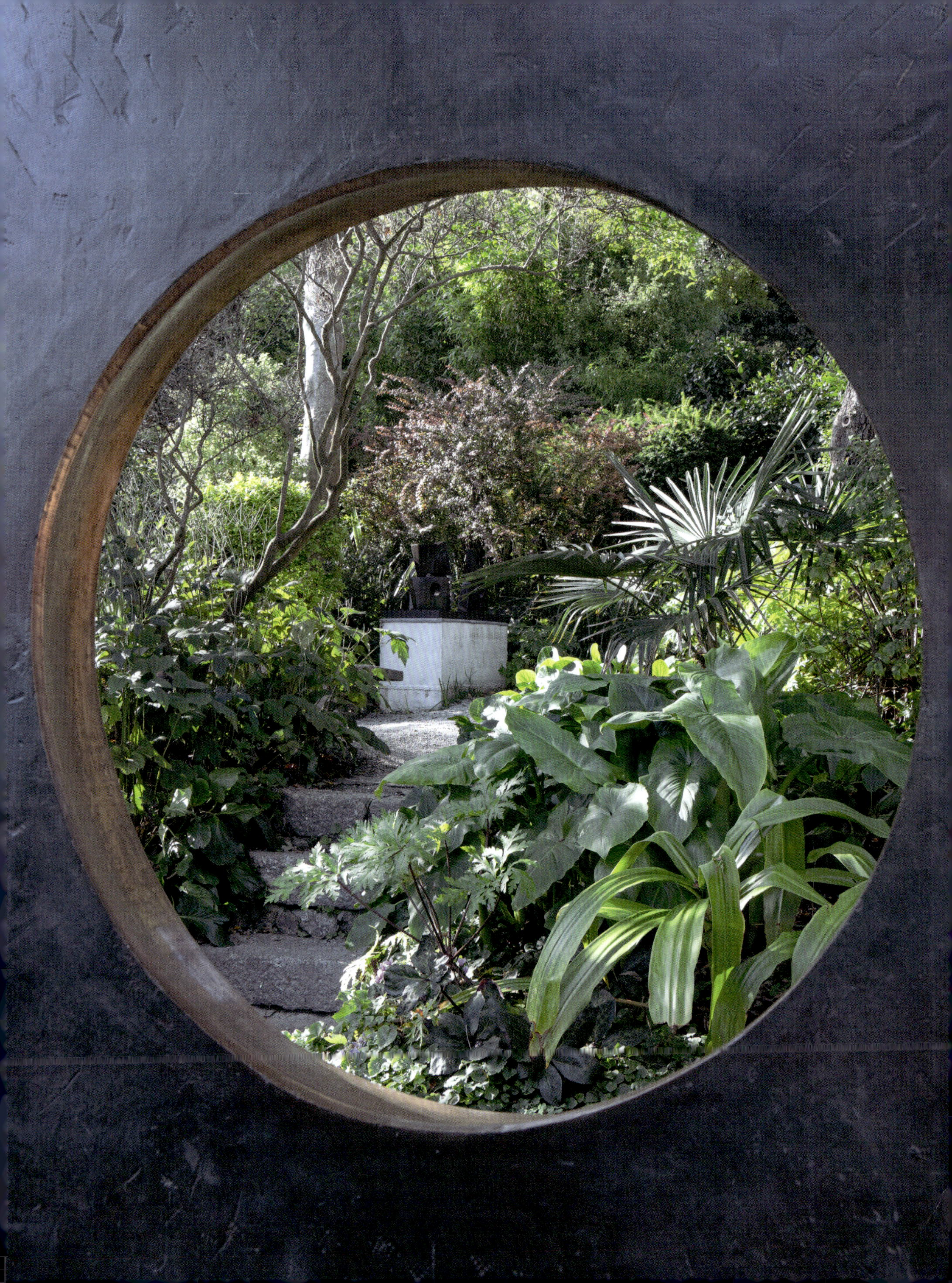

A Sort of Magic
Chris Stephens

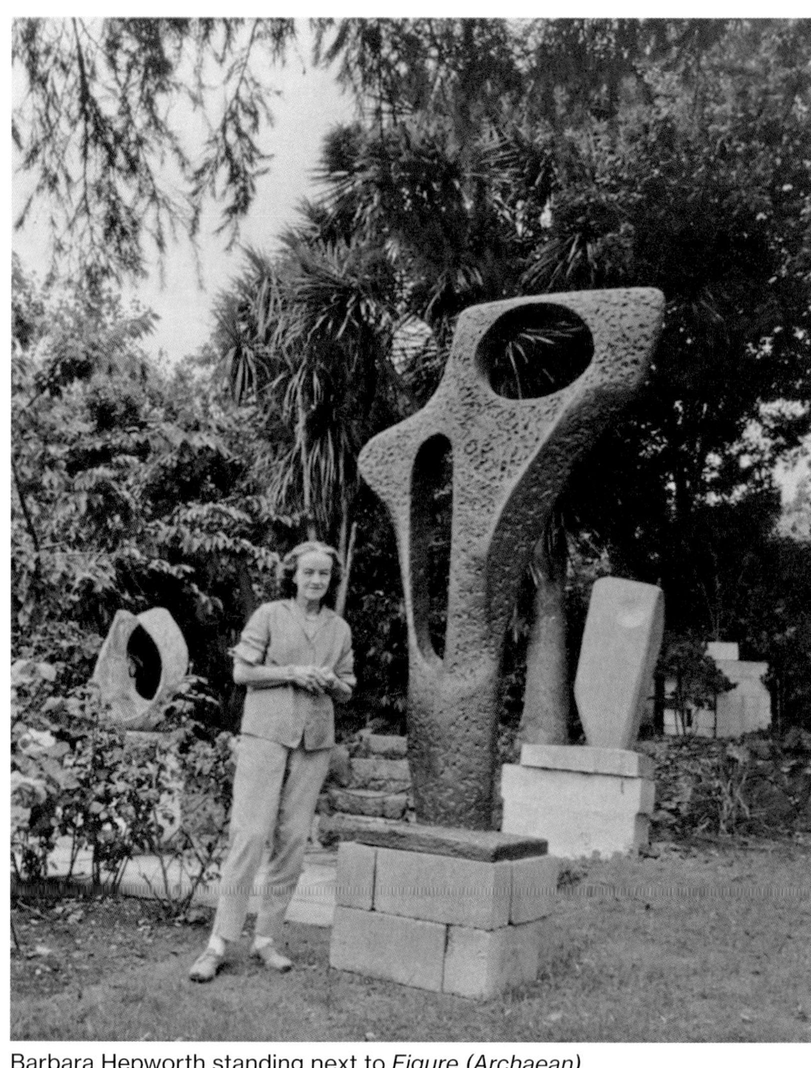

Barbara Hepworth standing next to *Figure (Archaean)* in Trewyn Studio garden, August 1962

'Finding Trewyn Studio was a sort of magic', Barbara Hepworth wrote of her St Ives studio.[1] Halfway up a steep, cobbled hill, hidden above the heads of passers-by behind high retaining walls, Trewyn Studio and its garden seemed then, as now, a secret haven amongst the tightly-packed houses and crowded narrow streets of old St Ives. There, for twenty-five years, Hepworth and her team of assistants produced sculptures in wood, stone, metal and plaster for bronze. As Trewyn became an attraction for collectors and critics from around the world, the garden was drawn into the presentation and reception of the artist's public image. Though essentially a private space, this was not simply a back garden, nor even a working yard, but an essential part of Hepworth's creative process and of the message she wished to convey with her sculpture. Hepworth's garden helped to secure the association of her apparently abstract works with the natural world. Its exotic planting and location in west Cornwall, with its sub-tropical climate and clear light, served to link her to a Mediterranean sensibility that was in contrast to orthodox British culture.

During the 1940s Hepworth had worked at Chy-an-Kerris, the home in nearby Carbis Bay that she shared with Ben Nicholson and their three children. This restricted both the number and size of sculptures she could produce and caused inevitable tensions between her roles as a wife and mother and as an independent artist. In 1949 her attention was drawn to the forthcoming sale of Trewyn Studio. The building and garden had, at one time, belonged to the large Trewyn House next door. With her growing reputation and increasingly strained family relations, she recognised the importance of the place, and decided to bid on the property with financial assistance from old friends including Helen Sutherland and Marcus Brumwell. Hepworth recalled: 'The first bid was far beyond my figure, and, according to my friends, I went pale green and fainted–so the bidding went on and I got the place…there I was–space, air, sun and a real proper workshop. The children had their own quarters just opposite and Ben his own big studio, and we all began to expand and grow.'[2] Though originally intended as a place purely for work, within a year Trewyn became Hepworth's home when divisions in the family proved irreparable and she and Nicholson separated and eventually divorced. Despite her growing fame and affluence, Hepworth remained in this modest studio until her tragic death in a fire there in May 1975.

It is unclear now how much of the present garden was already laid out when Hepworth moved to Trewyn in 1949. As part of the grounds to the big house, it was certainly cultivated, and some of the existing trees were already in place. Many others she planted herself, including a magnificent magnolia and flowering cherry. Photographs from the early 1950s suggest a rectilinear plan already interspersed with sculptures.[3] In 1965 an extra strip of land, at the top of the garden, was purchased from the sculptor John Milne, then the occupant of Trewyn House. Shortly before Hepworth's death, she placed the multi-part *Conversation with Magic Stones* 1973 on the far corner of this land.

How Hepworth conceived the relationship between the garden and her sculpture is uncertain. According to her secretary, Brian Smith, the place was not intended to be a 'sculpture garden' for public use, and though a visiting collector might be invited to stroll around, Hepworth rarely sold work from it. This was 'her own private garden with examples of her own work for her own enjoyment'.[4] Plants were chosen according to the artist's preference, though they also complemented the sculptures. Foliage was important as it provided a good background to the works. The style of the sculptures' presentation was simple–they were erected on the easily-moveable breezeblock piles on which she sometimes carved. How deliberately they were sited is also subject to question. It is most likely that she took considerable care over this in the early days, but practical factors may have impinged upon the overall design. From 1956, Hepworth cast more works in bronze than she made unique carvings. As each bronze edition included an additional cast reserved for the artist, the number of works needing a home greatly increased. In 1961, she acquired the former Palais de Danse across the road to provide extra storage as well as additional working space. Nevertheless, several stone carvings stayed in the garden and Hepworth seems to have tended to place larger bronzes there too. From the mid-1960s, poor health–including cancer and a broken hip that caused lasting pain– hampered her mobility and management of the studio. This, perhaps, was one reason why the sculptures in the garden accumulated. While the pieces we see now are generally where they were placed in her lifetime, before the garden opened to the public numerous works were removed,[5] including *Family of Man* 1970, a group of nine man-size totemic figures. This gives some indication of how over-crowded the place had become.

As well as a garden, this was also a working space. As soon as Hepworth acquired Trewyn, two huge blocks of limestone, which would eventually stand as *Contrapuntal Forms* beside the Dome of Discovery at the 1951 Festival of Britain, were positioned in the small concrete patch in front of a shed. Her turntable, with blocks of marble waiting to be carved, indicates how carving continued there until her death. In the early days she carved wood in the studio and worked on stone alongside her assistants in the garden. In 1957 a large shed was rebuilt as a workshop, which is now preserved largely as it was left at her death. The assistants' overalls–each with their own colour–hang on the door, while an array of points, claws, hammers and rasps gives a sense of how the stone was worked. It was only late in life that Hepworth allowed the limited use of power-tools. Next door, the plaster workshop is dominated by an unfinished cast of the wooden sculpture *Oval Form (Delos)* of 1955. Fragments of other works can also be seen: against the back wall the plaster for *Maquette (Variation on a Theme)* – a work related to *Garden Sculpture (Model for Meridian)* 1958 outside–stands to the right; to the left of the mirror are stacked plasters for three forms that were designed for the exterior of the John Lewis department store in London's Oxford Street but never used (a maquette is in the house). Unfinished pieces demonstrate how the plaster was applied to a chicken-wire armature, modelled when wet and then carved and smoothed when dry. Though they were occasionally exhibited, plasters were not seen as works in their own right but as models from which an edition of bronzes would be cast. In the top greenhouse are three plasters–*Sea Form (Porthmeor)* 1958, *Square Forms (Two Sequences)* 1963–4 and *The Family of Man, Figure 8: The Bride* 1970.

The juxtaposition of the plasters with the collection of cacti highlights a point of obvious formal comparison. Hepworth's work was, essentially, linked to nature: either its shape might have derived from a natural form or, more conceptually, it may have been determined by an idea of the organic, of growth or form. In this way, several of the sculptures in the garden–*Corymb*, say or *Meridian*–integrate themselves with the flowers and bushes around them. Though it became more dominant from the 1940s, this organic aesthetic had always been an aspect of Hepworth's art. Similarly, she had long sited sculptures out-of-doors. Two large works of the 1930s were positioned in gardens in Hampstead–her own and that of the artist, writer and collector Roland Penrose; both were damaged by wartime bombing. During the war, Hepworth photographed sculptures–her own and those of Naum Gabo–against the backdrop of St Ives Bay, radically repositioning their constructivist aesthetic. After the war, however, this dialogue between art work and nature came to the fore. Though she aspired to siting works in the

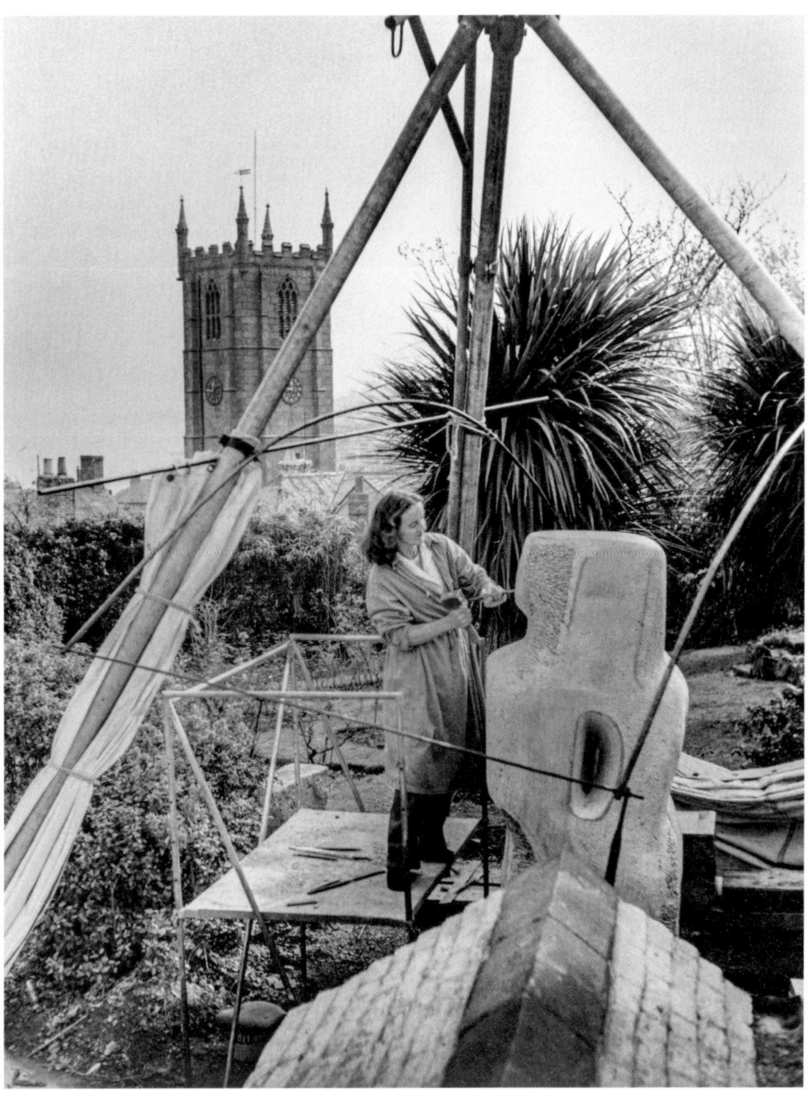

Barbara Hepworth carving *Contrapuntal Forms* in 1950

landscapes (as Henry Moore managed to do), the garden at Trewyn became the principal location for this exchange, as the forms and textures of plants and sculptures provided a complement and a counterpoint to each other.

Hepworth used her situation in Trewyn in the presentation of her work to the public. Many of her sculptures were photographed with evocative backgrounds. The most notable example is an image of the artist reaching up in the dawn half-light to finish off the plaster for *Cantate Domino* (which translates as 'Sing unto the Lord') against a backdrop of the tower of the parish church. Some works appear monumental set against the rooftops of St Ives; others are integrated with the sea-view. Thus, Hepworth's home and workplace became tied up with her public image as an artist. This became especially true in the early 1960s, when catalogues and articles included photographs of the artist seated in the garden surrounded by her work. Now there are only a few stone sculptures in the garden and the majority are bronze. Then, when she was new to metal casts, the display was a range of stones of different colours, textures and densities. Surrounded by foliage, it might have looked as if these were some sort of early monoliths emerging from the landscape. Hepworth's friend, the critic J.P. Hodin, identified one

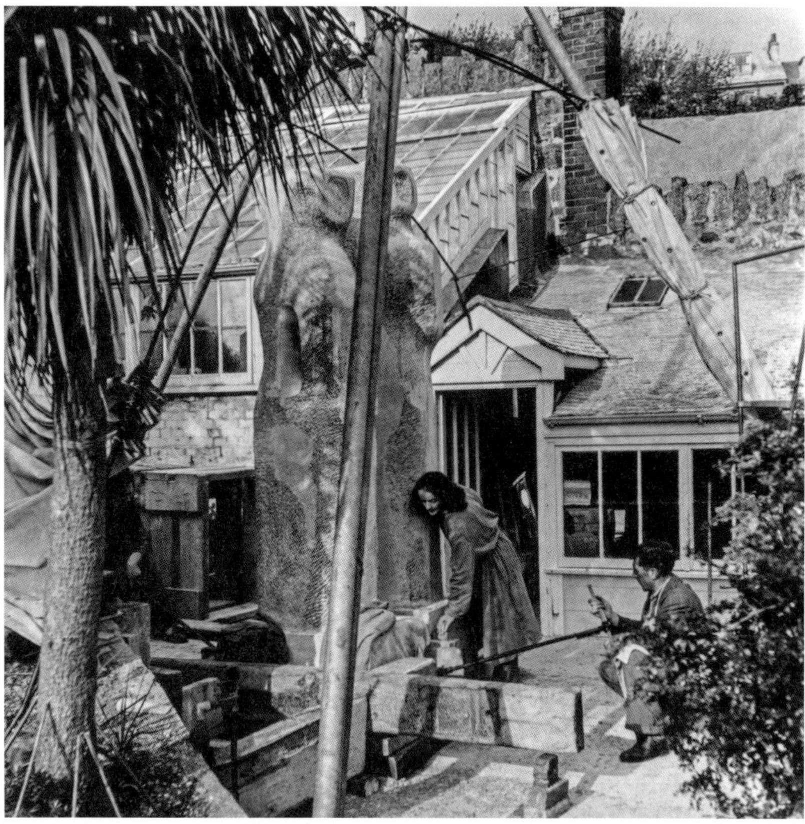

Denis Mitchell, Barbara Hepworth and John Wells at work on
Contrapuntal Forms, Trewyn Studio, 1950

material in particular that resonated with this special location and linked the sculptor to a more exotic place: white marble. He wrote:

We were sitting in the garden of Barbara Hepworth's Trewyn Studio. It was a late afternoon in the summer, the sky was blue, the bells of the nearby church sounded clear in the warm air… one could hear from afar the mighty roar of the waves… Under palm trees and flowering shrubs, between roses and gladioli some work of this outstanding English sculptor stood in the open. Nowhere in England had the sprit of the Mediterranean embodied itself so generously… I remarked that we might be sitting in Greece or in Southern Italy… so unmistakeably classical was the marble, the light and the sound of the South.[6]

Though she later realised that marble cannot be kept out of doors in the British climate, Hepworth concurred:

I love marble specially because of its radiance in the light, its hardness, precision and response to the sun. All this I learned to appreciate in Italy when I was a young student, and to have found this spot in Cornwall where nature corresponds so genuinely to my concept of style and my whole feeling has for years been a deep source of joy and satisfaction.[7]

Trewyn Studio and its garden provided the private space in which Hepworth was able to produce an extraordinary body of work. Almost inevitably, the garden and sculpture became locked into a creative dialogue. Just as that integration of art with nature created a peaceful environment for the artist, so it has helped to secure her posthumous reputation.

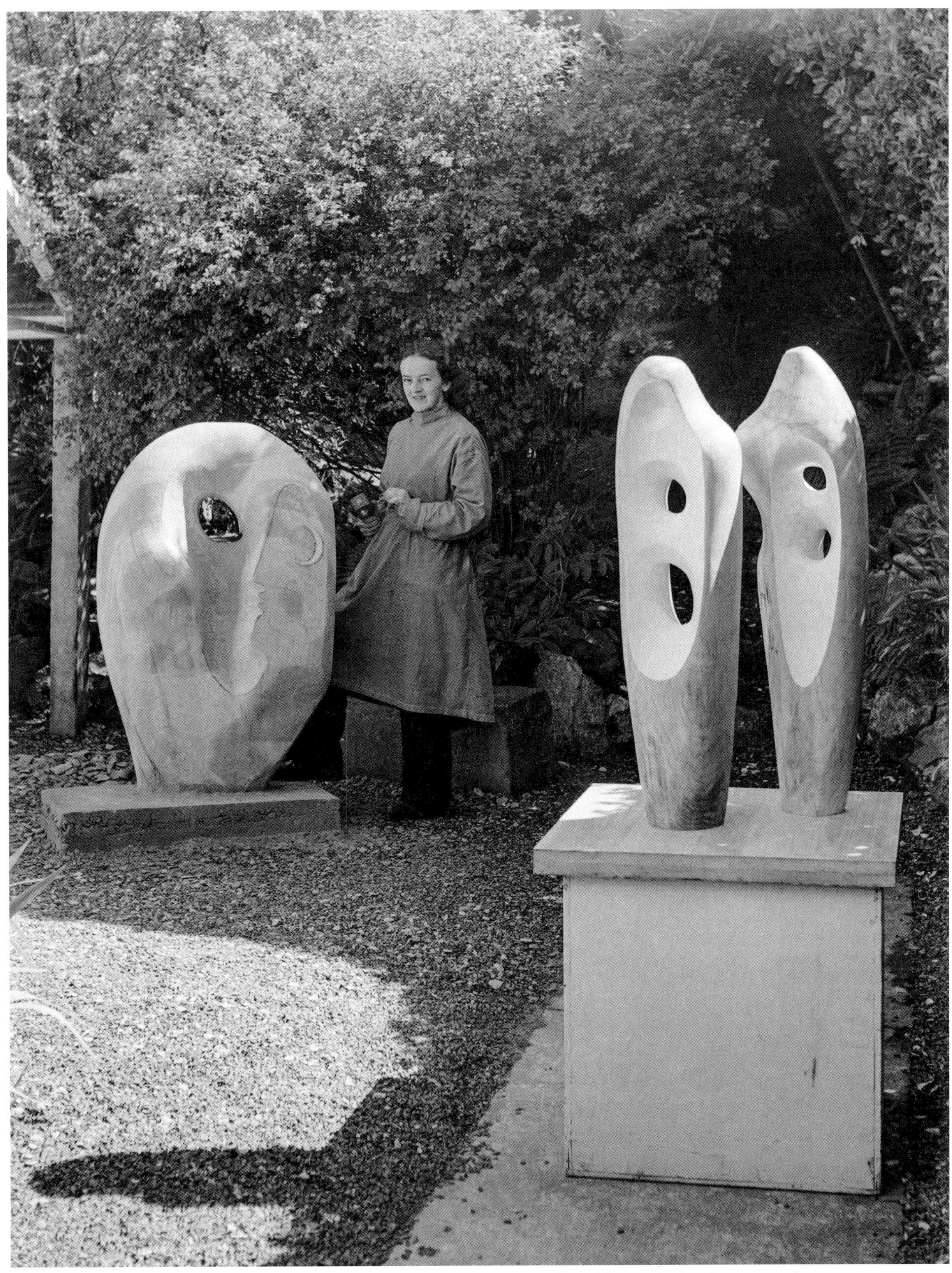

Barbara Hepworth standing beside *Biolith* at Trewyn in 1949, with *Two Figures* in the foreground

Trewyn Studio
Barbara Hepworth's Garden in St Ives
Miranda Phillips

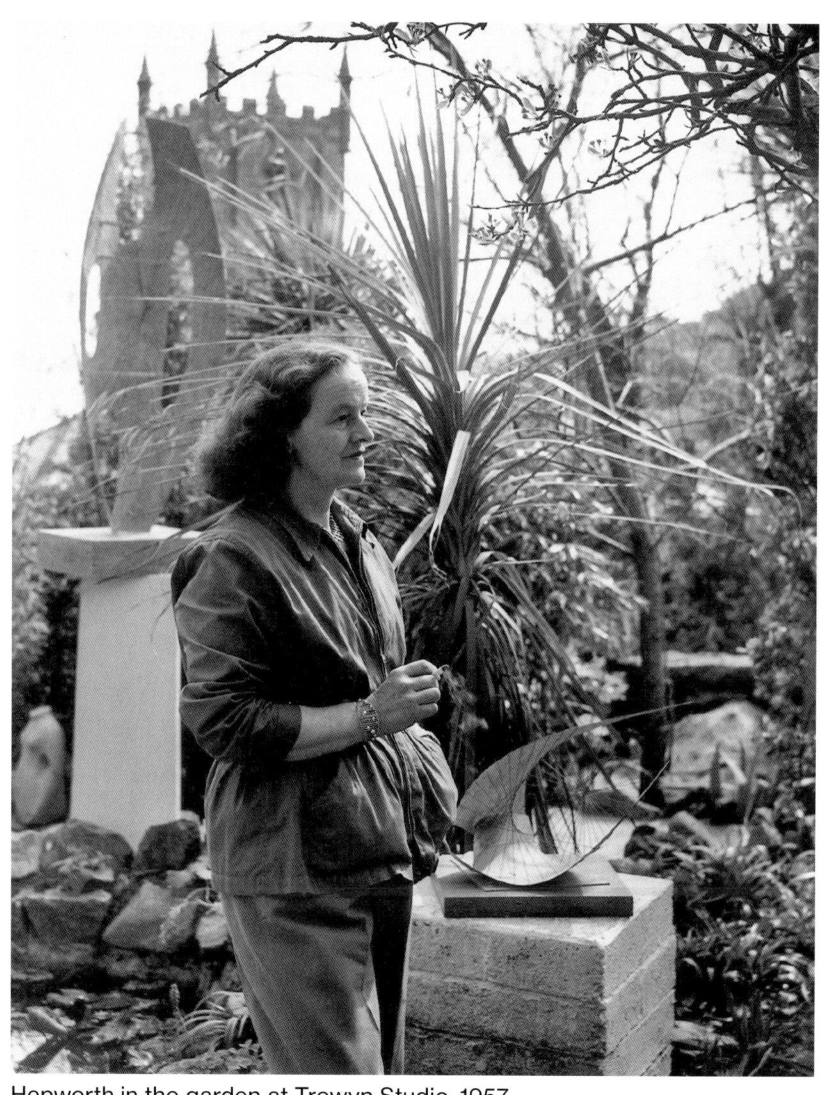

Hepworth in the garden at Trewyn Studio, 1957

When Barbara Hepworth came to Cornwall in August 1939, she could little have thought that she would spend the rest of her life in the area. She and her husband, the painter Ben Nicholson, had left London hurriedly as the threat of war and of the bombing of the capital drew closer. They were particularly anxious for the safety of their three young children, triplets Simon, Rachel and Sarah. Initially staying with friends Adrian Stokes and Margaret Mellis at their home in Carbis Bay, just outside St Ives, Hepworth and Nicholson quickly moved into the first of two houses they rented in Carbis Bay during the war years. Through this period of hardship and self-reliance, Hepworth's determination and capacity for hard physical work were devoted to providing for her family. At first she worked in the Stokes' market garden; later, at Dunluce, their first rented house, she ran a small nursery school which allowed her to earn a little, provide a service and educate her children.

Hepworth turned the garden over to vegetables during the wartime 'Dig for Victory' campaign and was awarded a local certificate for the quality of her produce. The soil in the area was fertile and free draining, and she learnt rapidly which plants would thrive and which would prove less successful. Ben reported in letters to friends that Barbara had harvested more than 600 tomatoes and an exceptional crop of Brussels sprouts in the first six months.[1] In 1942 they took a seven-year lease on a larger house, Chy-an-Kerris. Here, at last, was extra living space for a growing family. Although she did not transform the garden into a vegetable plot, she had already developed a valuable working knowledge of horticulture, on which she drew to transform the garden of her next and final home.

Towards the end of the 1940s, Hepworth and Nicholson began to look for separate studio and living spaces within St Ives. Throughout 1948 the local newspaper, the *St Ives Times*, reported St Ives Town Council's proposal to purchase Trewyn House and its estate, and it may have been the public outcry generated that first alerted Barbara to Trewyn Studio, which was built on the eastern end of the Trewyn House estate.[2] The Council planned to turn the gardens and orchard into a public car park, and it was this that caused the most objections. In March 1948 the issue was resolved shortly after the Council's Compulsory Purchase Order was refused on appeal to the Department of the Environment. The Council for the Protection of Rural England offered £25 towards buying local plants for a new public garden on the site through their local representative, Will Arnold-Forster.[3] The remaining two-thirds of the estate–Trewyn House and some mature garden and the smaller Trewyn Studio with its small garden area – were to be sold at public auction.

Hepworth had often walked past the high granite walls of Trewyn with her shopping, unaware of the hidden studio and garden within. The auction notice described the property as a 'stonebuilt studio premises and garden (of particular interest to artists and others) 30' 3" × 21' 9" [9.2 × 6.6 metres], having store and two wc's underneath, with two separate entrances. Attractive front Rose Garden with lean-to Greenhouse and store.'[4] Hepworth's move to Trewyn Studio marked the start of an entirely new way of living, for at last she had the time, space and peace required to devote her considerable energy to sculpture. The children were at boarding school for most of the year, Nicholson acquired a studio no more than five minutes walk away, and Trewyn Studio, with its high surrounding walls, offered privacy yet stood within the busy artists' community of St Ives.

Part of Hepworth's philosophy as an artist was 'to infuse the formal perfection of geometry with the vital grace of nature', and, with her abiding love of landscape, she had always drawn inspiration from the natural world.[5] Photographs of her Hampstead studio before the war show potted plants among the sculptures; many years later, pictures taken in her St Ives studio show the same casual integration of plants and works in progress. Soon after Trewyn Studio became her home, Hepworth added plants to her working environment. A set of photographs from 1950 illustrate this: terracotta pots overflowing with lemon-scented pelargoniums share shelf space with files and chisels; crassulas (Jade plants) and house-leeks contrast with blocks of marble.

For the first few years composer and friend, Priaulx Rainier was the primary source of energy in transforming the garden with Hepworth, and her knowledge of plants proved to be vital in conceptualising its layout. When Hepworth arrived, the space was a traditional rose garden with palms, shrubs and several mature trees. Just as she set about re-envisaging the spaces of the studio for her own use, so she did with the garden and the upper workshop, in the latter of which some early additions were bougainvillea, plumbago and heliotrope, the scents of which Hepworth recalled in her letters.[6]

Hepworth worked on two major commissions for the Festival of Britain of 1951: *Contrapuntal Forms* made from Irish Corrib limestone and *Turning Forms*, a reinforced concrete structure. She rigged up spotlights so that she could continue carving the massive blocks of limestone well into the night and also installed a canvas shelter made by a local sail-maker, which protected the work during the wet July of 1950. Hepworth and her assistants frequently worked ten to fourteen-hour days in the studio[7] but it wasn't until 1951 that Hepworth 'felt a primary & creative urge to do something about the garden.'[8]

Rainier, who had been helping on the garden from 1950, and who shared her belief in the revitalising, calming influence of nature, offered to help. Later they would organise musical and arts events together in St Ives, including the St Ives Festival of 1953. Both, too, were acquainted with men who had major horticultural interests. Hepworth had known Will Arnold-Forster since his intervention in the public-garden controversy in 1948. On visits to his home, Eagles Nest, set high on the hills above Zennor village, Hepworth was impressed by the marvellous garden he had created. She owned a copy of his classic book *Shrubs for the Milder Counties*, which had been published by Country Life Books in 1948.[9] Reading this and observing the wild plants about her, Hepworth's thoughts about gardening on this coastal fringe of Cornwall would have been confirmed; mild winters and the warming effects of the Gulf Stream were balanced by the bite of salt-laden winds that only plants adapted to coastal conditions could survive. Rainier had known the plant-hunting Viscount Chaplin of Totnes since they were music students together. His travels had included botanical expeditions to New Guinea; the planting ideas Rainier had assimilated from his estate and her familiarity with the plants of her native South Africa may have added to the range of plants Hepworth considered for Trewyn Studio. Hepworth also visited the Isles of Scilly and enjoyed the sub-tropical planting schemes established there from the 1850s, which illustrated how successful adventurous gardening plans could be.

Hepworth's copy of *Shrubs for the Milder Counties* has passages underlined in pencil and notes added in the margins beside certain plant descriptions. Tucked inside the front cover are two sheets of notepaper bearing Hepworth's distinctive handwriting. They appear to be a 'shopping list' for plants she was considering for Trewyn Studio, and many of these plants still flourish in the garden today.

Heading the first sheet is a list of trees already present: 'Dracaena–7 or 8 very large, Copper Beech, Holly, 2 pear trees, 2 or 3 elm (severely lopped)'. Beneath this is a note stating that the County Council had agreed to plant deciduous trees 'right up to Richmond Place', which formed part of the boundary between the public and private gardens. Scattered over the rest of this sheet and the next are the names of trees and shrubs being considered including *Hoheria sextylosa, Myrtus luma*, one large rowan tree,

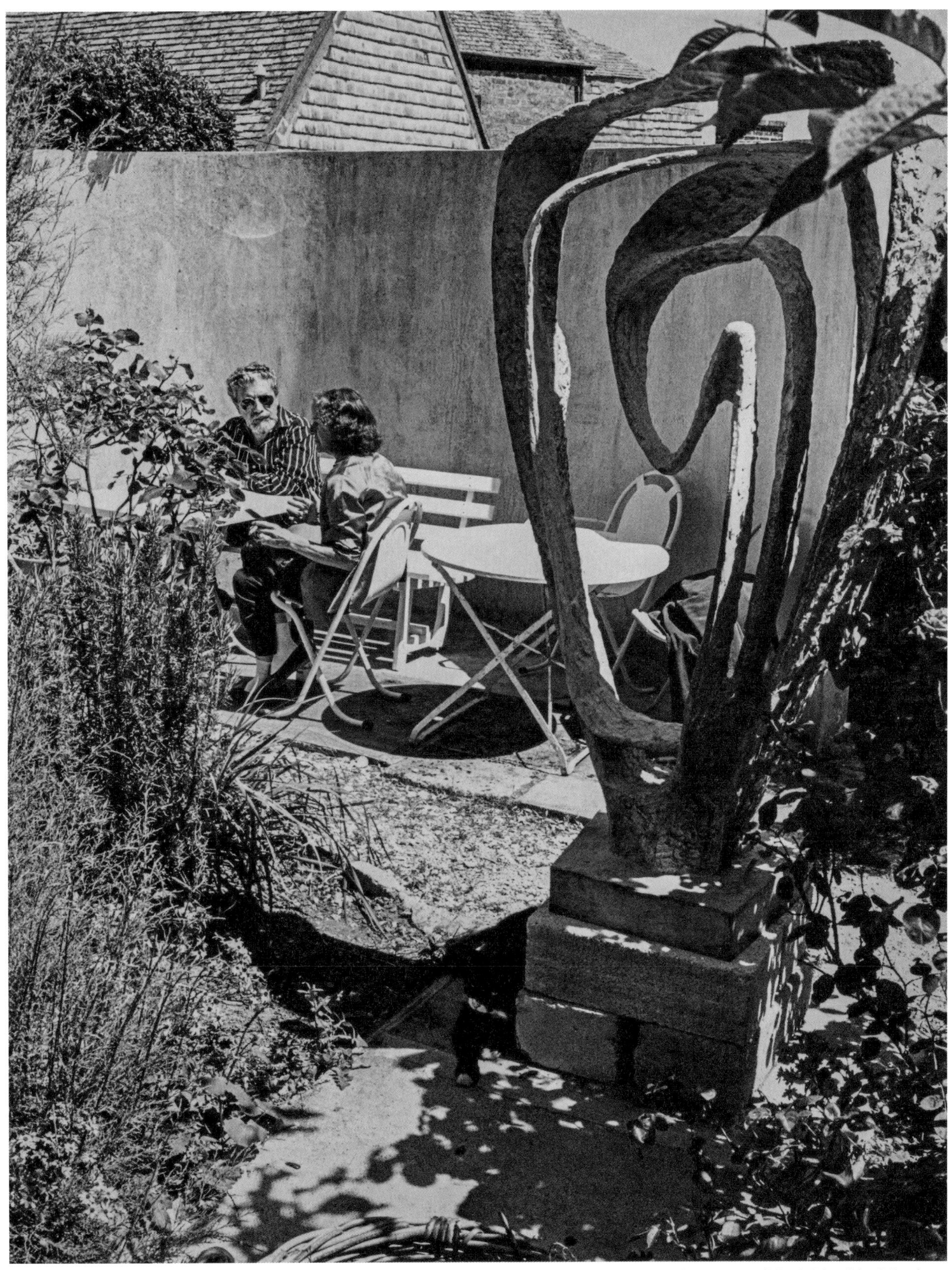

Barbara Hepworth with the art critic Mervyn Levy at Trewyn in 1962, with *Garden Sculpture (Model for Meridian)*

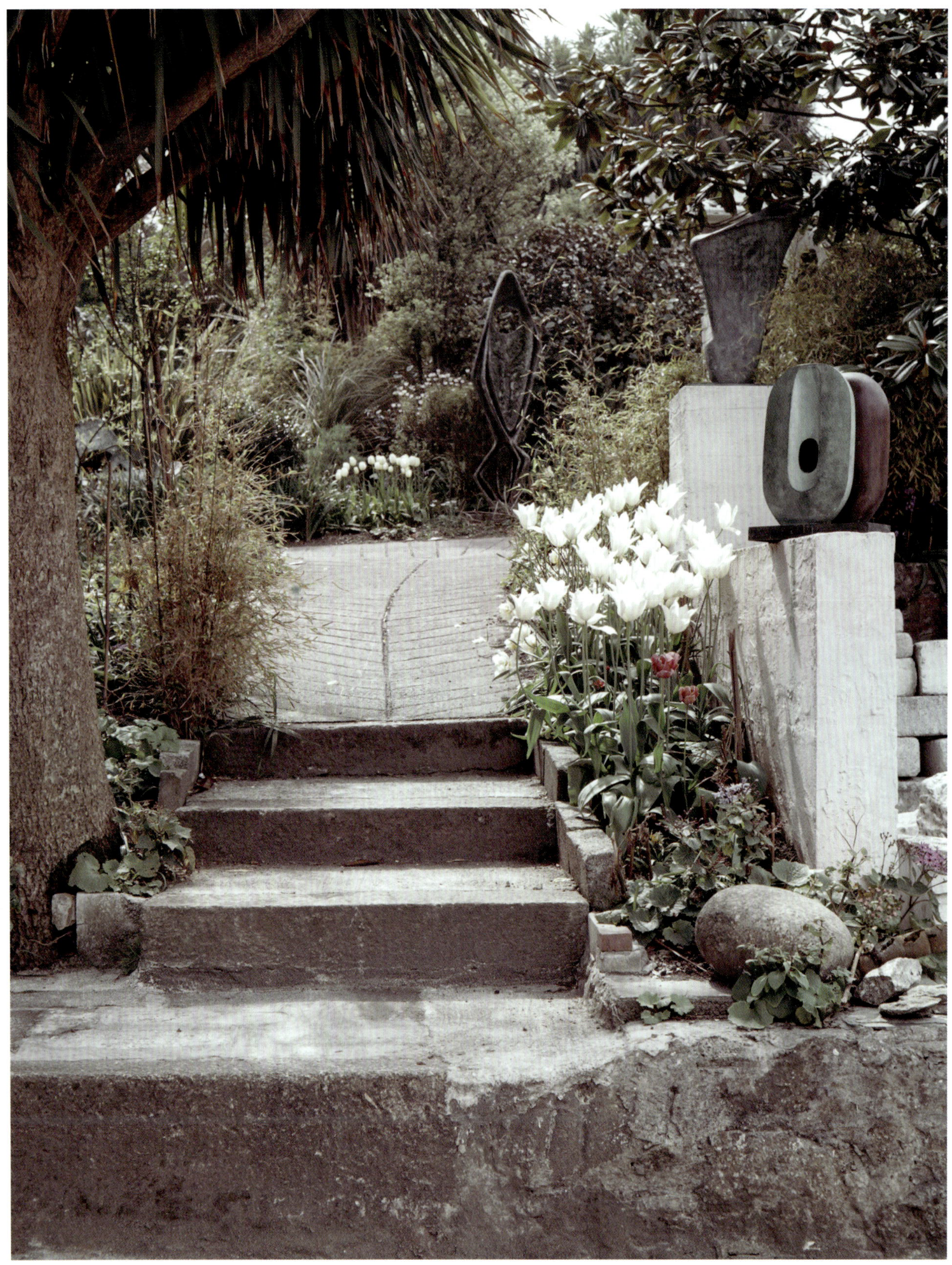

Trewyn Studio garden, 15 May 1969

one magnolia *(grandiflora)*, mimosa, eucalyptus and *Magnolia stellata*. The telephone number for Treseders Nursery is noted and circled, and an interesting feature is that the current prices of some trees are included. During these earlier years, she set about removing original plants such as geraniums and dahlias and altogether changed the character of the garden.

By 1955 the original trees combined with her new additions, Hepworth joked she had turned the space into 'more a forest than a garden. Cats lurk. Sculptures are hidden.'[10]

At this point, having produced a substantial body of work during her first few years at Trewyn Studio, Hepworth re-visited the layout of the garden. Facing south-east, it was an irregular square, sloping gently upwards to the fence and low, crumbling wall that separated it from the grounds of Trewyn House. Several mature trees and some overgrown shrubs sheltered the southern edge of the plot. The lawn was scrubby and worn, and roses bloomed raggedly, dropping their petals amongst tangles of purple and blue cinerarias. Hepworth entered negotiations with her neighbour at Trewyn House, John Milne, and they agreed to redraw the boundary 'in a straight line instead of a curved line'.[11]

A document to this effect was signed in December 1956, witnessed by the painter Alan Lowndes and Rainier.[12] Hepworth's accompanying letter explained that Denis Mitchell could draw the boundary with string that afternoon, revealing her eagerness to start redesigning the garden immediately. Her letter continued, 'tomorrow and Thursday D[enis] M[itchell] and Keith [Leonard] could break the soil ready for Priaulx and I to plant over Xmas', concluding, 'I think my back isn't equal to digging therefore it would help to have K and DM' and 'I thought I might 'phone Treseders (a local plant nursery) for plants almost at once.'[13]

This smaller scale reworking of the garden started over Christmas 1956 and Denis Mitchell and Keith Leonard almost certainly did most of the digging, as Hepworth suffered intermittently from backaches. Turf, brought from a nearby building site, replaced the old lawn, but some of the roses were retained to be planted in two freshly cut, straight beds. The shallow pond was cleaned and reconstructed, and a decorative stone rockery added above it. Winter was not the ideal season in which to replant, but fortunately there were no severe frosts that year and very few plants seemed to suffer adversely.

Over the next five or six years, extra plants were added: the Chusan or Chinese fan palm *(Trachycarpus fortunei)*, *Fatsia japonica*, two hibiscus, a bay tree and the New Zealand satin flower *(Libertia grandiflora)* and a hedge of mixed planting including *Fuchsia* and *Euonymus japonicus*. Two varieties (one of which still remains) of honeysuckle were set to sprawl over the rockery beside the pond and the lovely, scented water hawthorn *(Aponogeton distachyos)* planted to blossom in it. In summer, the ultramarine and purple daisyheads of *Pericallis* x *hybrida* 'Stellata' (florist's cineraria) bloomed and self-seeded, roses scented the air and tall blue agapanthus flowered. The garden paths meandered, presenting new views at every turn. The changing light conditions enhanced the sculptures that Hepworth had placed on breezeblock plinths amongst the flowers and foliage. The small, white-painted summerhouse was an earlier addition from 1951 – a place to relax and enjoy the peace of the garden, the bustle of the town temporarily forgotten.

In 1959 Barbara Hepworth approached John Milne to discuss buying a section of his garden, a move that would give her more space to display her work. A letter dated February 1959 enclosed her sketch-map, showing an addition of 3 feet 6 inches (1.06 metres) in depth on the south side of the garden, deepening to approximately 9 feet (2 .75 metres) on the opposite edge, adjacent to the carving studio. A greenhouse, occasionally used by Milne as an extra studio, was included, as were two trees, a holly and a pear.

The sale was not finalised until August 1965, probably as a result of the overriding need to work and exhibit, and the fact that Milne spent part of most years abroad. The new strip of land was considerably larger than what they previously discussed and increased the size of the garden by about half.[14] This new section was cleared of its overgrown shrubbery and planted with *Pittosporum*, spotted laurel and Berberis varieties, as contrasts of form and colour. Several favourite sculptures were placed at strategic viewpoints in this woodland atmosphere. The greenhouse enabled Hepworth to grow plants that were too tender to grow outside. Plumbago and a cerise bougain-villea scrambled up the inner wall, whilst agave, aloe and a number of cacti shared shelves and the red-tiled floor.[15] Towards the end of her life, in 1973, this area of the garden became home to a glade of bamboo, surrounding *Conversation with Magic Stones*, in the south-west corner, whose massive forms were delicately contrasted on the other side of a pathway by the slender, ethereal *Apollo* 1951. The breeze, whispering though the bamboo, makes this a peaceful, meditative spot.

In 1967, a fall on holiday in the Isles of Scilly resulted in a fractured hip that restricted Hepworth to a wheelchair for several months; thereafter she often used a walking stick for support. Some of the long recovery period was spent planning subtle changes in the garden. Photographs taken in the spring of 1969 show the main pathway bordered with stately white tulips, a gift from Holland. A small stone bridge constructed over the pond reamins in the garden today but the tulips were temporary additions–Hepworth felt they were too formal for her essentially 'natural' garden. In 1968, Hepworth and her old friend, the potter Bernard Leach, were awarded the Freedom of the Borough of St Ives and Hepworth was created Bard of the Cornish Gorsedh, with Leach receiving the same in 1975 – extraordinary honours for citizens who were not Cornish natives.[16] As a response Hepworth opened Trewyn Studio garden to the people of St Ives, something she had done regularly over the years. From time to time a writer or admirer was person-ally invited to tea in the garden, when Hepworth would urge them to 'Wander round the garden alone. Let them [the sculptures] look at you and they'll speak to you',[17] but it was usually Hepworth's domain, with her family, staff and cats the only visitors. The garden would have been particularly lovely for the public opening, with drifts of white Japanese anemones surrounding the late roses. The upper part of the garden had honeysuckle and the first crinums' white trumpets; amongst the shrubs at the top of the garden were sprays of vibrant orange crocosmia and young spikes of berries on the Lords and Ladies *(Arum italicum)*. The flowers and foliage both emphasised and provided counterpoint to the forms of Hepworth's sculptures.

Dame Barbara Hepworth died in 1975, leaving instructions about Trewyn Studio in her will. Her family and executors fulfilled her wish to turn the house and garden into the small museum that continues to fascinate so many visitors. Over 14,000 people visited during the first year.[18] The museum staff, all of whom had worked for Hepworth, cared for the garden for some years but lacked the horticultural expertise to maintain it under such pres-sure of numbers. In 1984 the nurseryman and gardener John Anderson offered his services. With a lifetime's experience and knowledge, and a sensitivity to the vision of Hepworth's garden, he painstakingly restored its beauty. The exceptionally cold winter of 1987 killed the two *Hoheria sexty-losa* that Hepworth had planted and caused some of the cordylines and phormiums to die back to ground level, but judicious replanting filled such gaps. Anderson only added plants that maintained the mood of the garden–informal, natural and relaxed rather than clipped and regimented–and preferred the natural control of pests and weeds in place of chemical methods. Hepworth would have approved; from her earliest years at Trewyn Studio she had been keen to attract wildlife–nest boxes were installed,

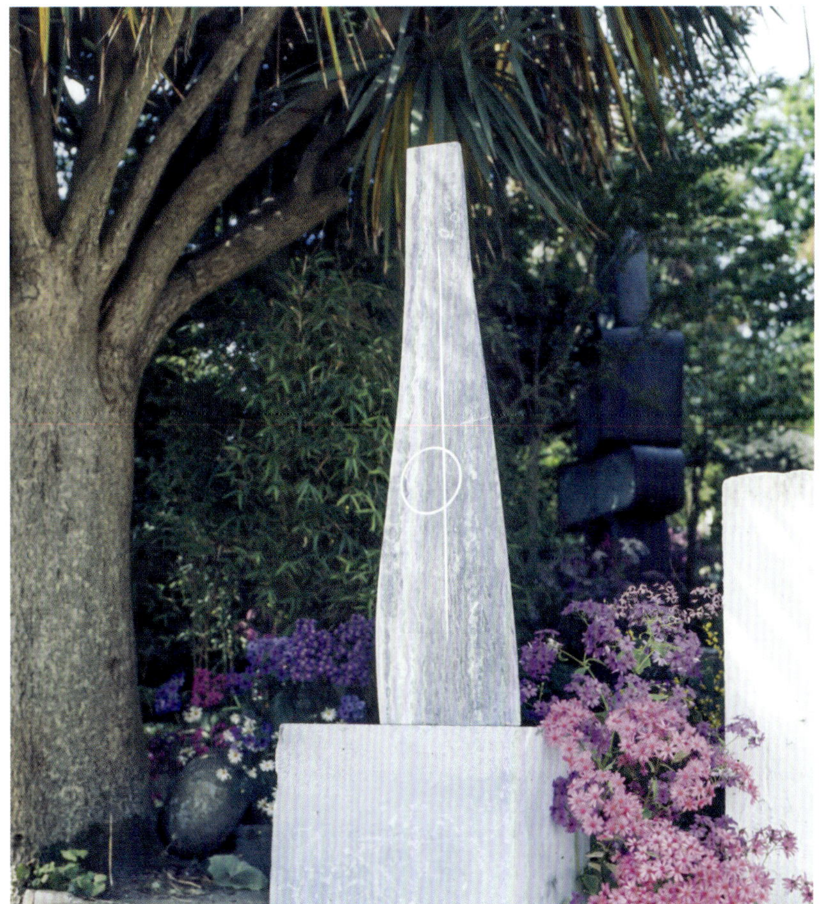
Trewyn Studio garden, with *Shaft and Circle* (Irish marble), in 1972

hopefully out of the reach of her pet cats.[19] Blackbirds, bluetits, sparrows and wood pigeons still visit regularly, drawn by seeds, fruit, insects and the pond. Redwings have been winter visitors in the past and hummingbird moths visit in September to feed on the *Salvia microphylla*. The omnipresent St Ives herring gulls perch and nest on the Studio roof but they prefer more open areas so are rarely seen in the garden itself.

In 1980 the Museum became the responsibility of Tate, their first venture outside London. The garden has matured and developed over the years, and the practice of replacing like with like has continued. In recent years some of the palms (*Cordyline australis)* have died under the canopy of taller trees, so have been replaced with the more shade tolerant Chusan palm *(Trachycarpus fortunei)*. Most recently, the responsibility for the care and sensitive management of the garden has been in the hands of Head Gardener, Jodi Dickinson, who has thoughtfully worked to keep the garden as Hepworth envisaged. The sheltering hedges on the eastern and southern boundaries are pruned regularly to reveal the view that Hepworth enjoyed from her garden: the Church tower, the rooftops of the town and the serene sweep of St Ives Bay beyond.

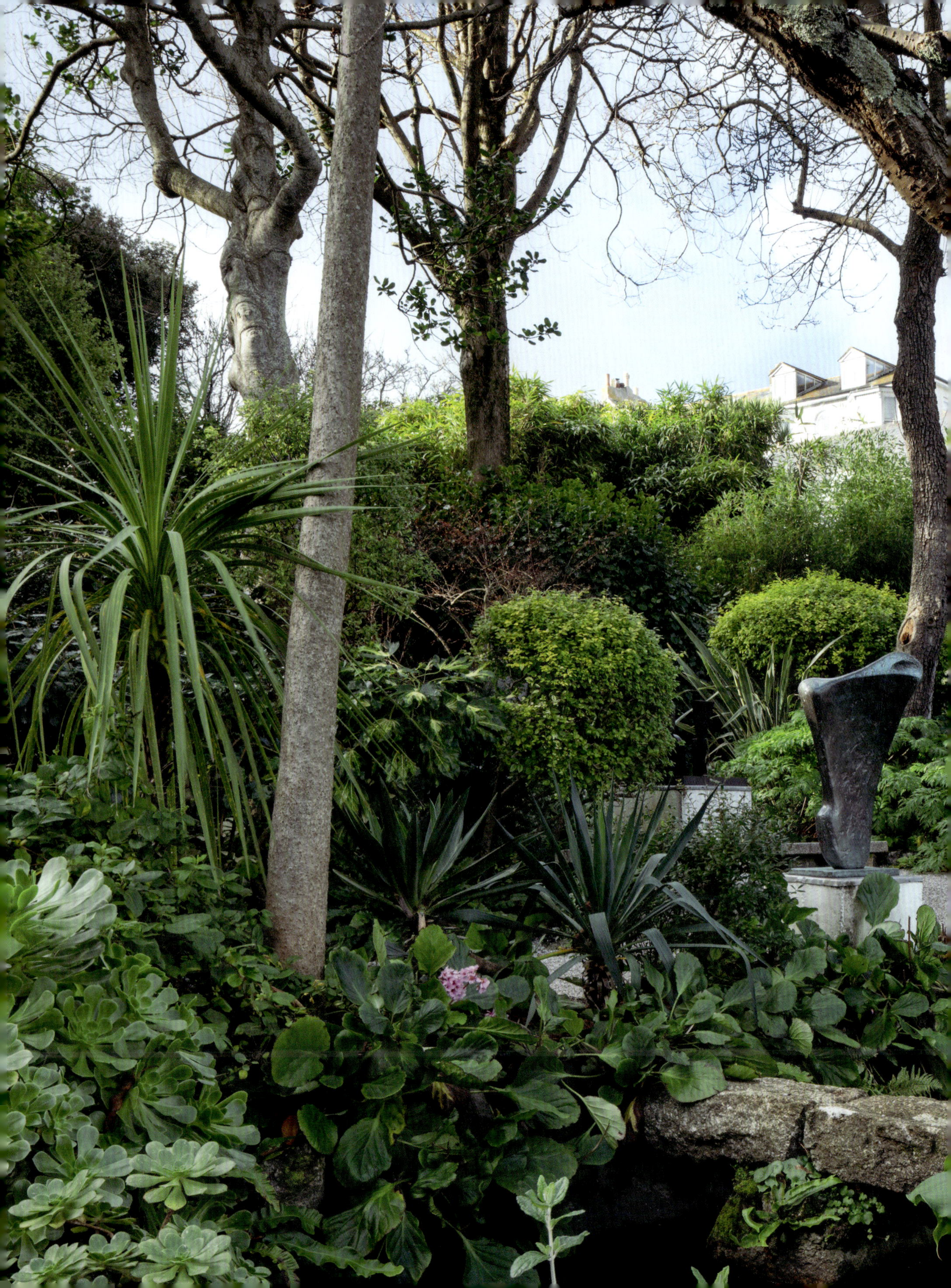

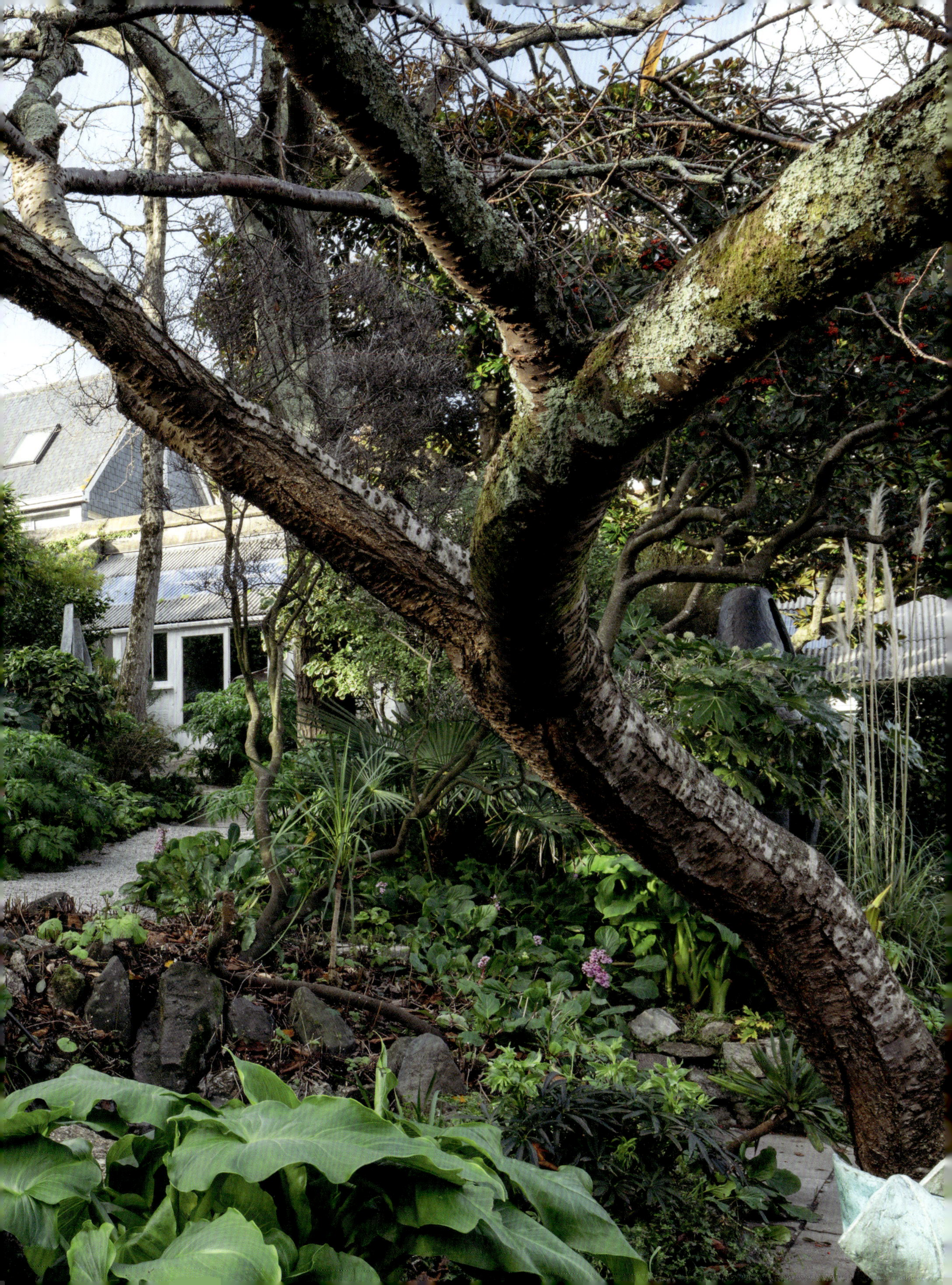

Spring

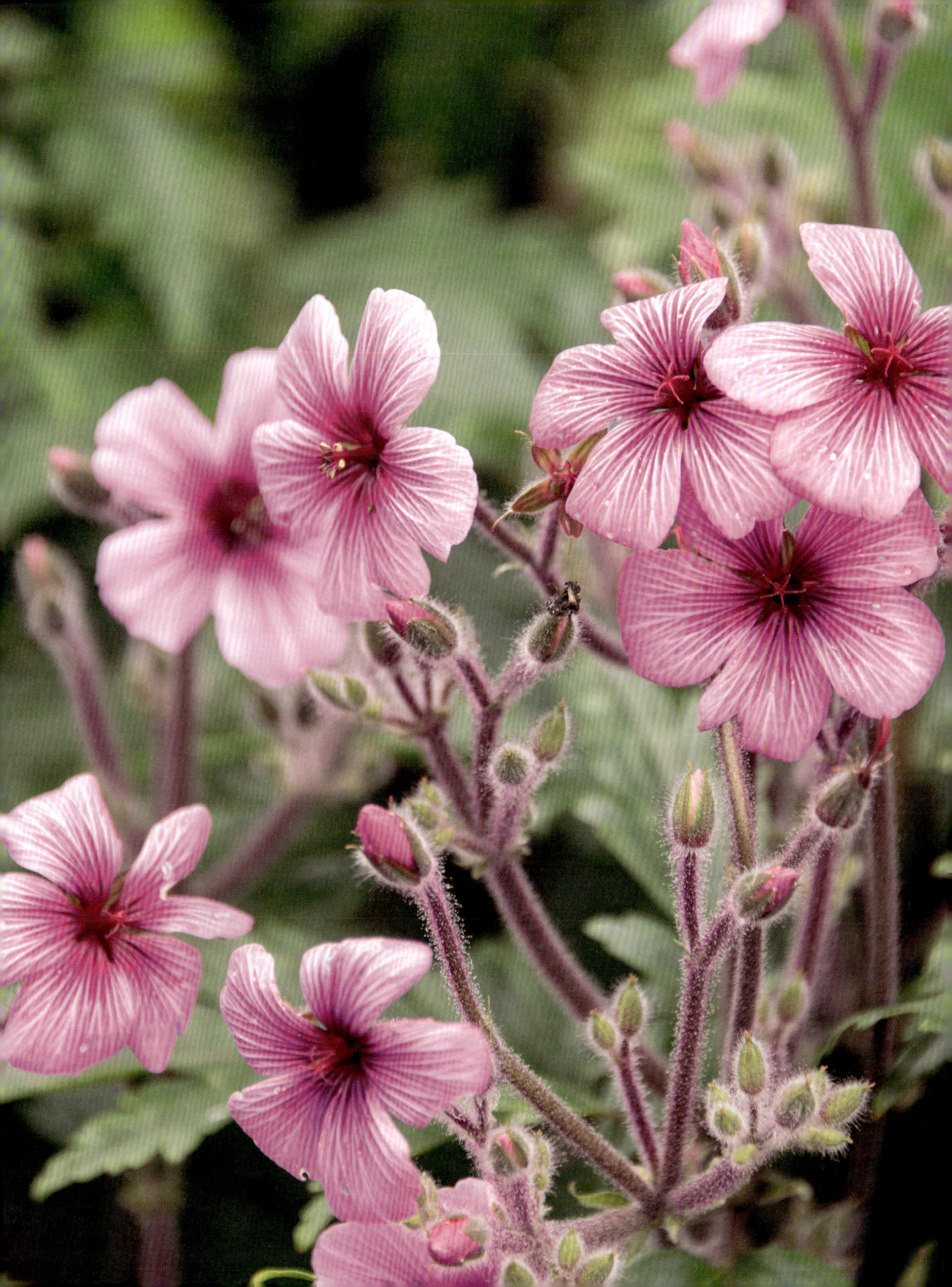

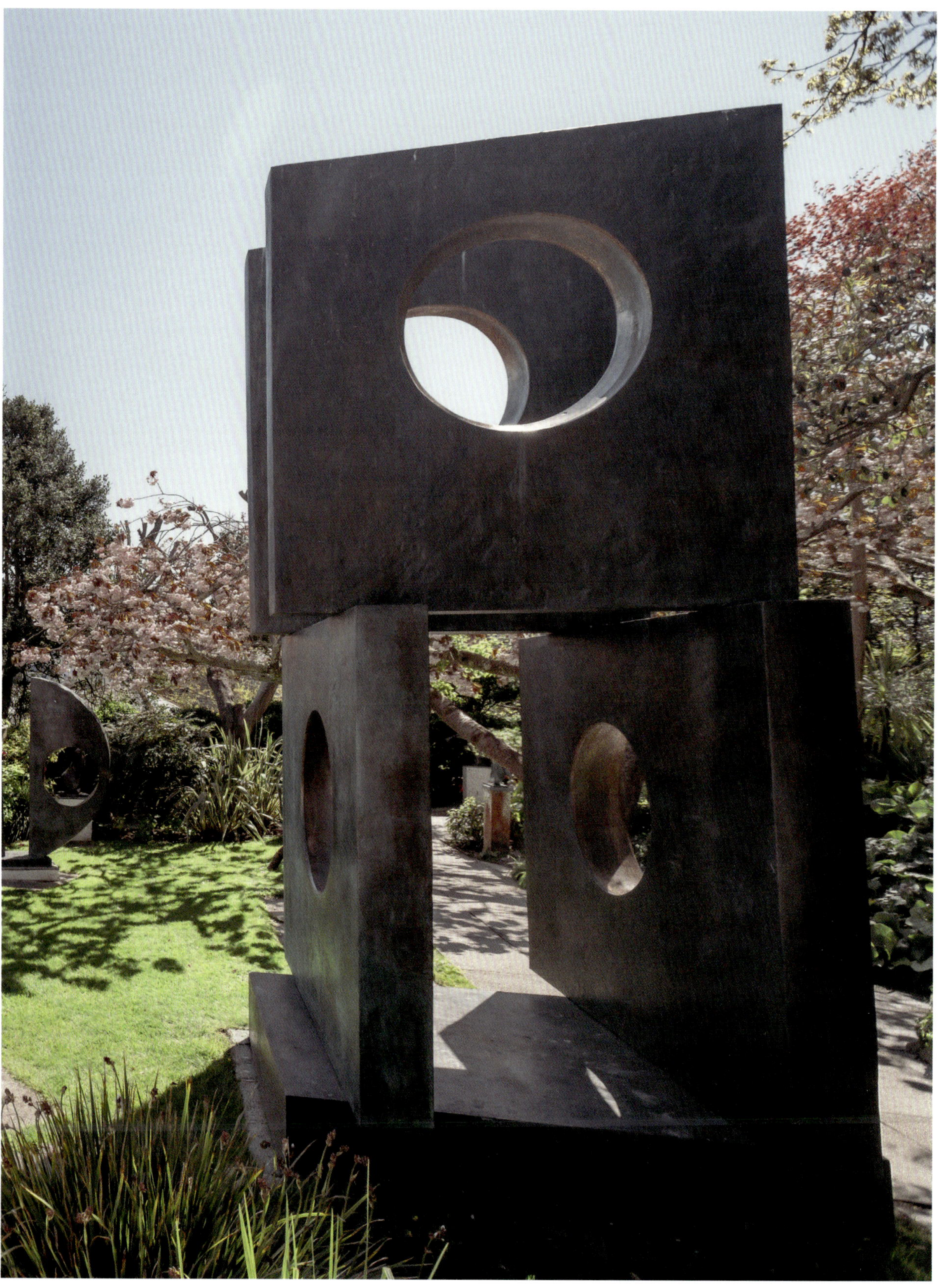

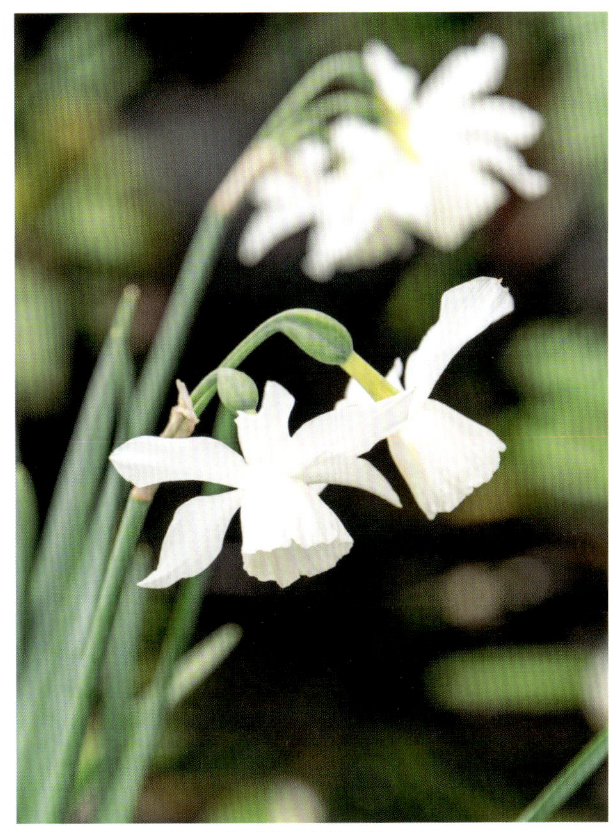

1 *Narcissus* 'Thalia' white daffodil

Four-Square (Walk Through) 1966 (left)
Hepworth's wish for the spectator to engage physically with sculpture reached its full realisation in this work, which invites us to pass through its middle. The circular apertures lighten the form and offer shifting views into and out of the sculpture. Despite the geometric structure, each vertical element and each hole is irregular in shape. Hepworth acknowledged that her desire to make such large works sprang from a sense of urgency caused by the diagnosis of cancer in 1965. This piece replaced a rose bed that once occupied the same position.

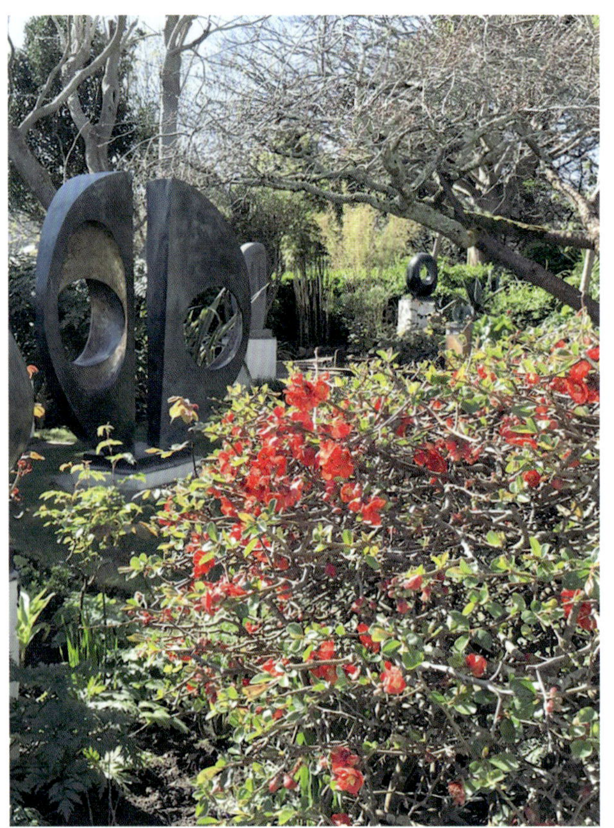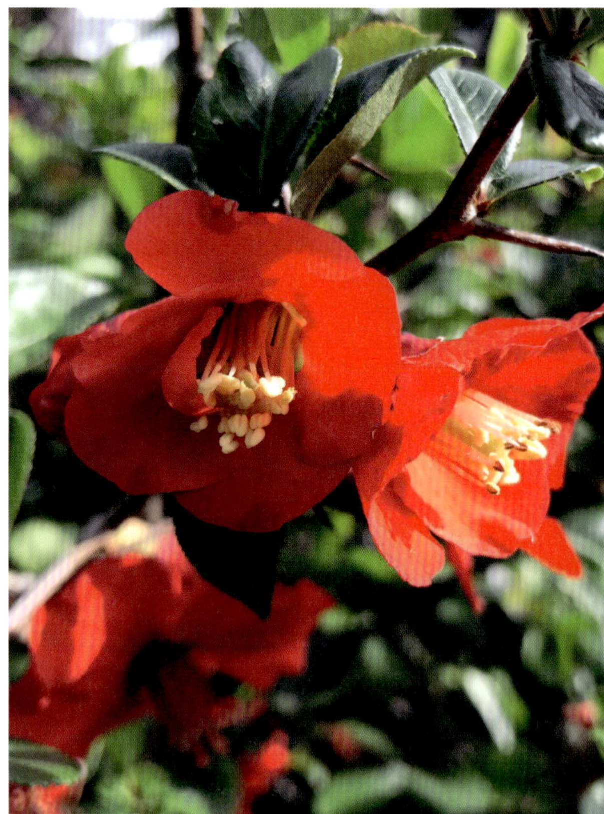

2   *Chaenomeles japonica* Japanese quince

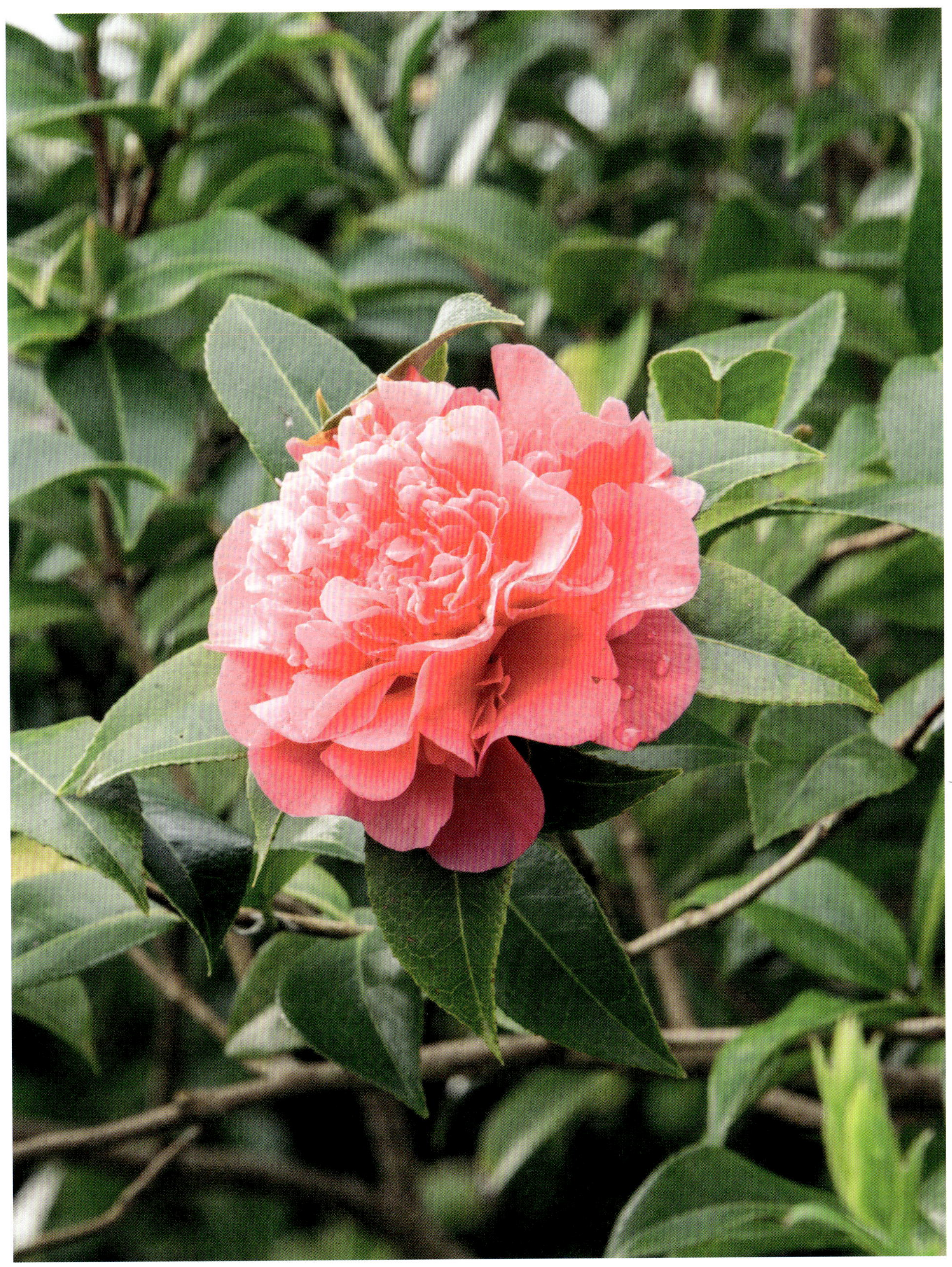

3 *Camellia japonica* common camellia

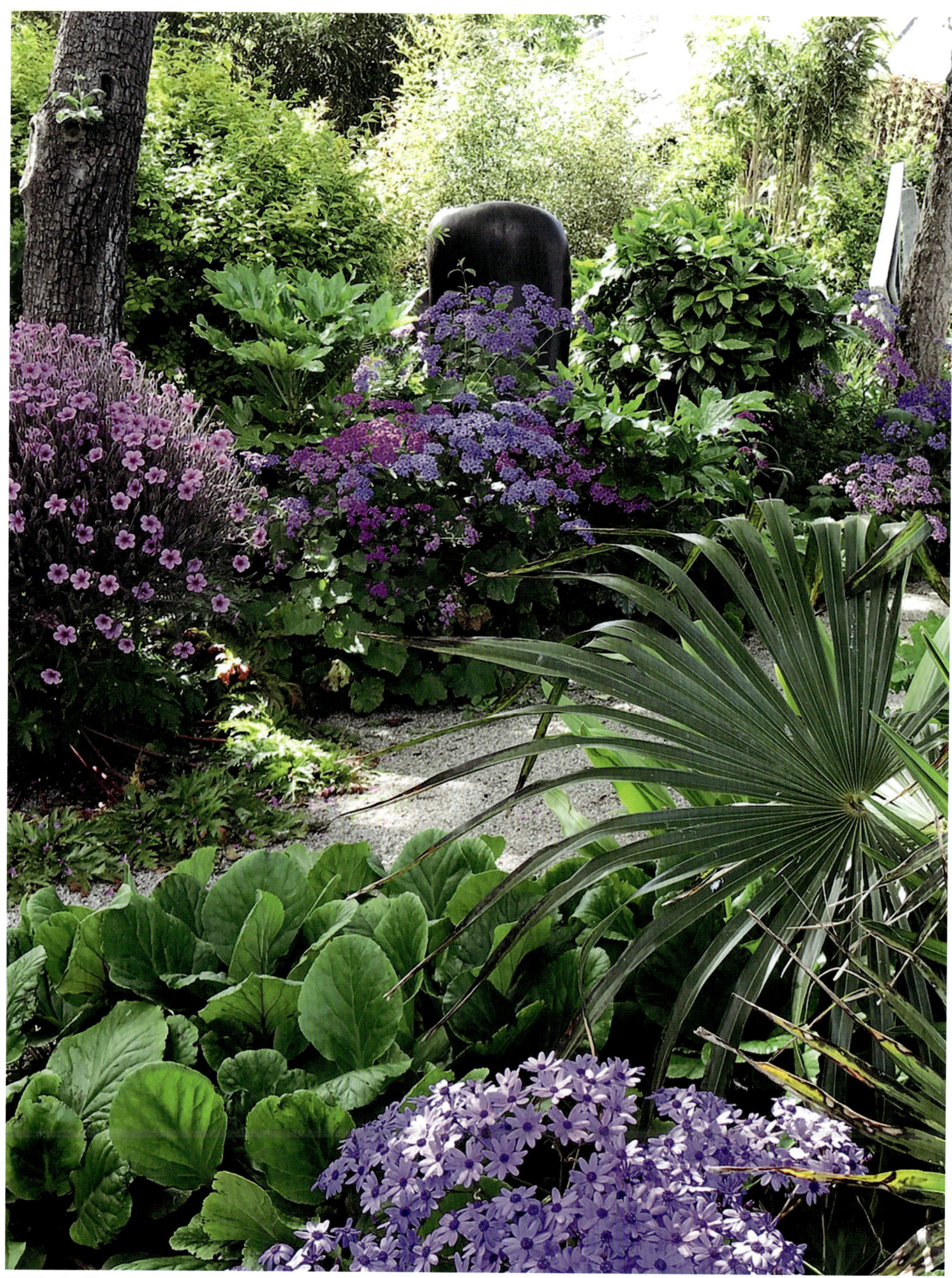

4 *Pericallis x hybrida* 'Stellata' florist's cineraria, see also cover

1 *Narcissus* 'Thalia' white daffodil
Although daffodils have been grown and developed in Cornwall for many decades, Hepworth chose to grow only one variety at Trewyn, *Narcissus* 'Thalia'. This variety, with its delicate, milk-white flowers, grows well in semi-shade, and so makes a beautiful yet subtle addition to the garden. *Narcissus* bulbs need well-drained sites, but soil type and position are not so important. In general, they should be planted in September, five to ten centimetres deep, depending on bulb size, to achieve the best results. Like most bulbs, they benefit from a thin layer of silver sand in the bottom of the planting hole to ensure good drainage. Flower heads can be removed once faded, then let the foliage die back naturally until June or July to nourish the bulbs.

2 *Chaenomeles japonica* Japanese quince
This early-flowering, deciduous shrub has scarlet red flowers with rounded petals and prominent anthers, which appear in masses of small clusters from March until May. Small apple-shaped, golden-yellow fruits develop very slowly during summer – when ripe they can be used to make quince jelly, but need protracted cooking to produce even a small quantity. Alternatively, add one or two to a fruit-bowl to perfume the whole room. The glossy, rounded, dark green leaves are shed in autumn to reveal mahogany-coloured branches set with thick, spiky thorns. Japanese quince will form an attractive, fairly compact shape in open positions, with some pruning, and can also be trained against a wall. Attractive to pollinators and capable of providing shelter to smaller birds within its dense spiky twiggy structure, *Chaenomeles japonica* is great for wildlife. Fully hardy, it likes good drainage and prefers a sunny position, but will tolerate light shade.

3 *Camellia japonica* common camellia
Originally from China and Japan, and plentiful throughout the historic gardens of Cornwall, camellias are named after the chemist Georg Joseph Kamel (1661–1706), who made a lifetime study of the flora of the Philippines. They are exquisitely beautiful plants – most form dense, upright shrubs with crisp, glossy, dark green leaves and delicate blooms. The flowers vary from an almost luminous white, through shades (and even streaks) of pink and red, to deepest claret. Forms range from the simplest of singles and doubles, to complex peony forms. They flower early, and buds can be damaged by frost or cold winds, which should be considered when choosing a planting site. Camellias also require an acidic soil; where the soil is alkaline or neutral, they can be grown in containers in an ericaceous and soil-based growing media. Pruning is only necessary to retain a neat shape and should be done after flowering.

4 *Pericallis x hybrida* 'Stellata' florist's cineraria
The cineraria is one of the most important plants for portraying the atmosphere that Hepworth created, because they feature frequently in the archival photos taken of the garden towards the end of her lifetime. The florist's cineraria are a biennial or short-lived perennial, slightly tender and enjoy a moist humus-rich soil; they are ideally suited to the woodland environment and maritime climate of the museum garden. At approximately three feet tall, this cultivar is very different from the unnaturally floriferous, short-lived, and compact 'Senetti' cultivar you might find in garden centres today. In fact, now incredibly rare, the florist's cineraria is currently unavailable to buy commercially in the UK. After being lost to the garden for many years a small population was rediscovered in a local garden, and then re-introduced in 2016. So, fortunately, it lives on to make the most wonderfully unique and atmospheric contribution. In May and June they light up the garden with a spectrum of harmonious colours from deep indigoes and violets, through to magentas, pinks and white. It makes for a particularly special experience and is now a firm signature plant at the Barbara Hepworth Sculpture Museum and Garden.

Image 1951–2 (right)
As the title suggests, Hepworth wished this work to stand for a generalised identity. She related *Image* to the notion of the figure in the landscape, and described such figures as 'powerfully rooted' and as creating the impression of 'growth and expansion… an image, or symbol of the span of time'. Implicitly, she was comparing her work to the ancient monoliths of West Cornwall.

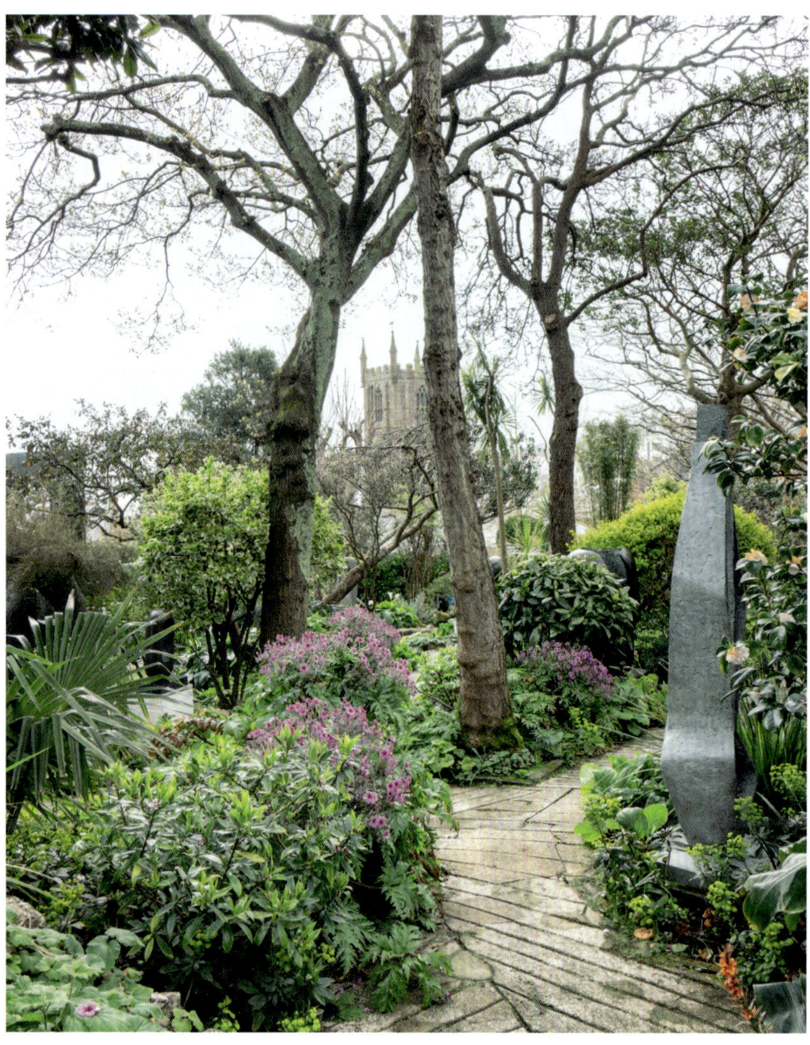

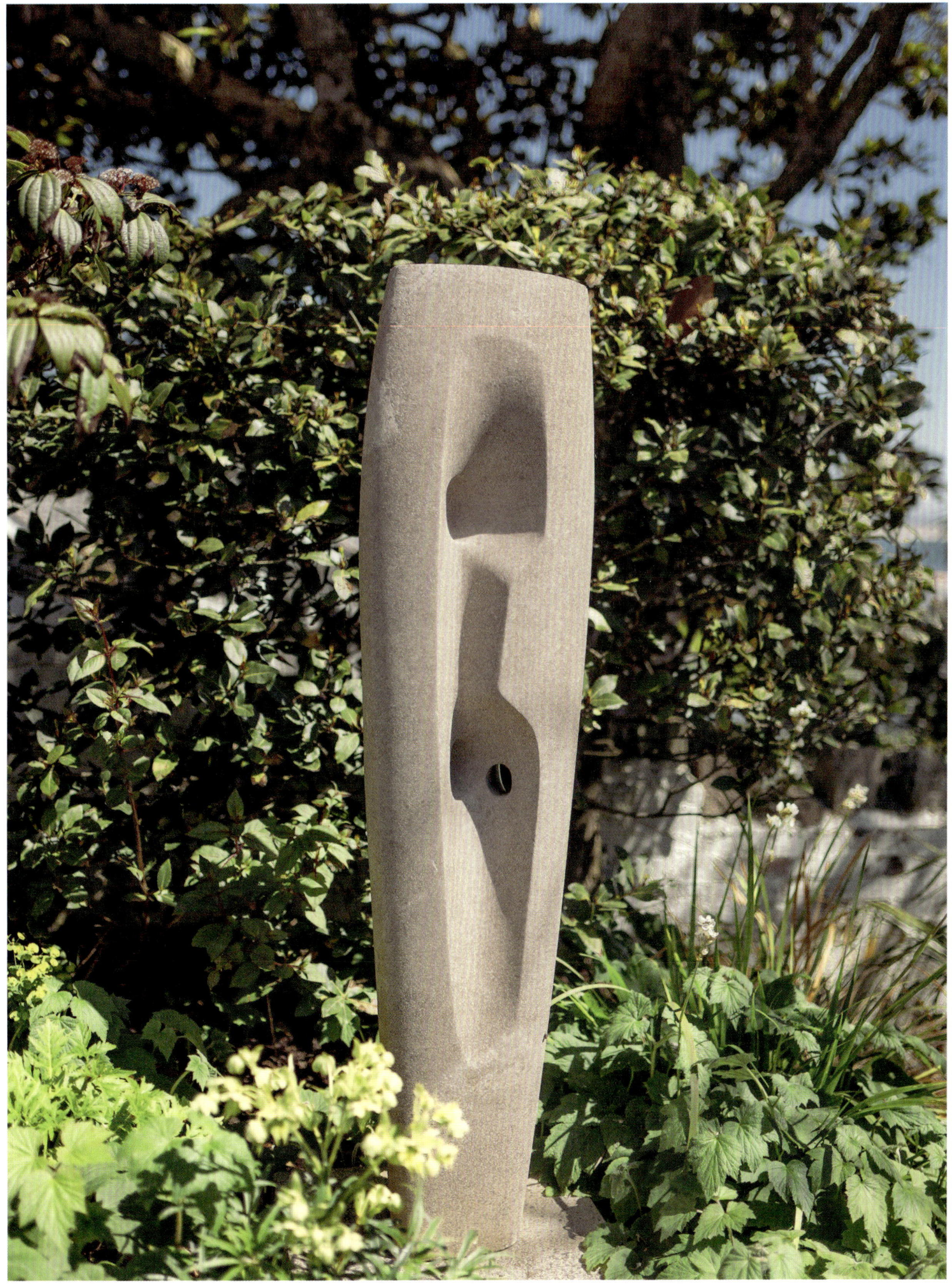

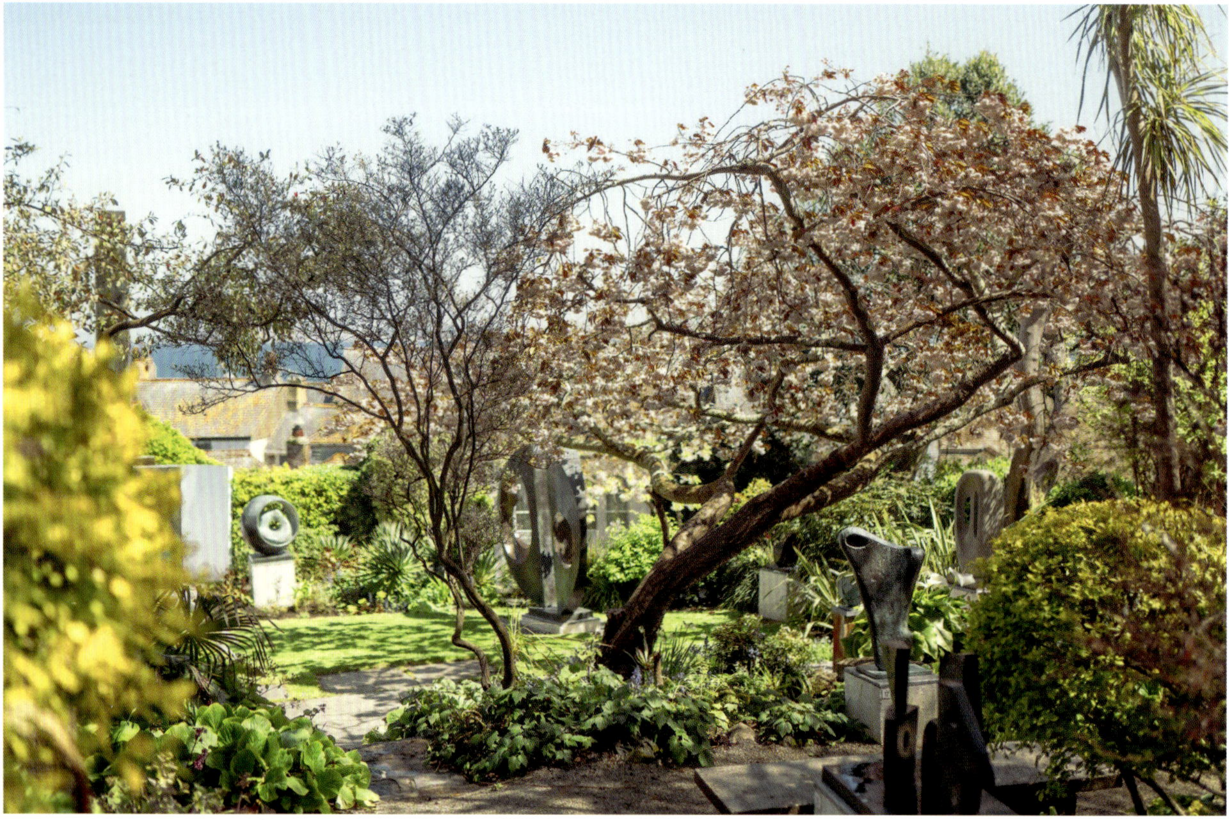

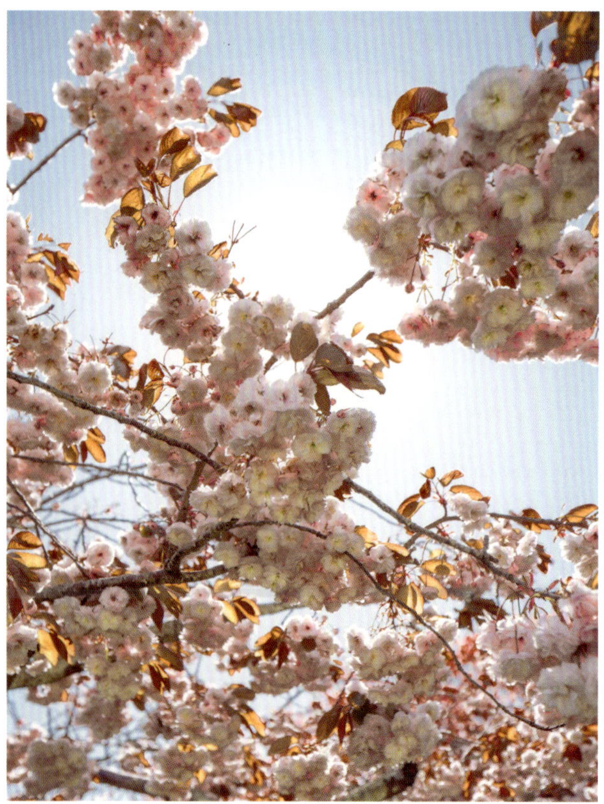

5   *Prunus* 'Accolade' cherry tree (and below)

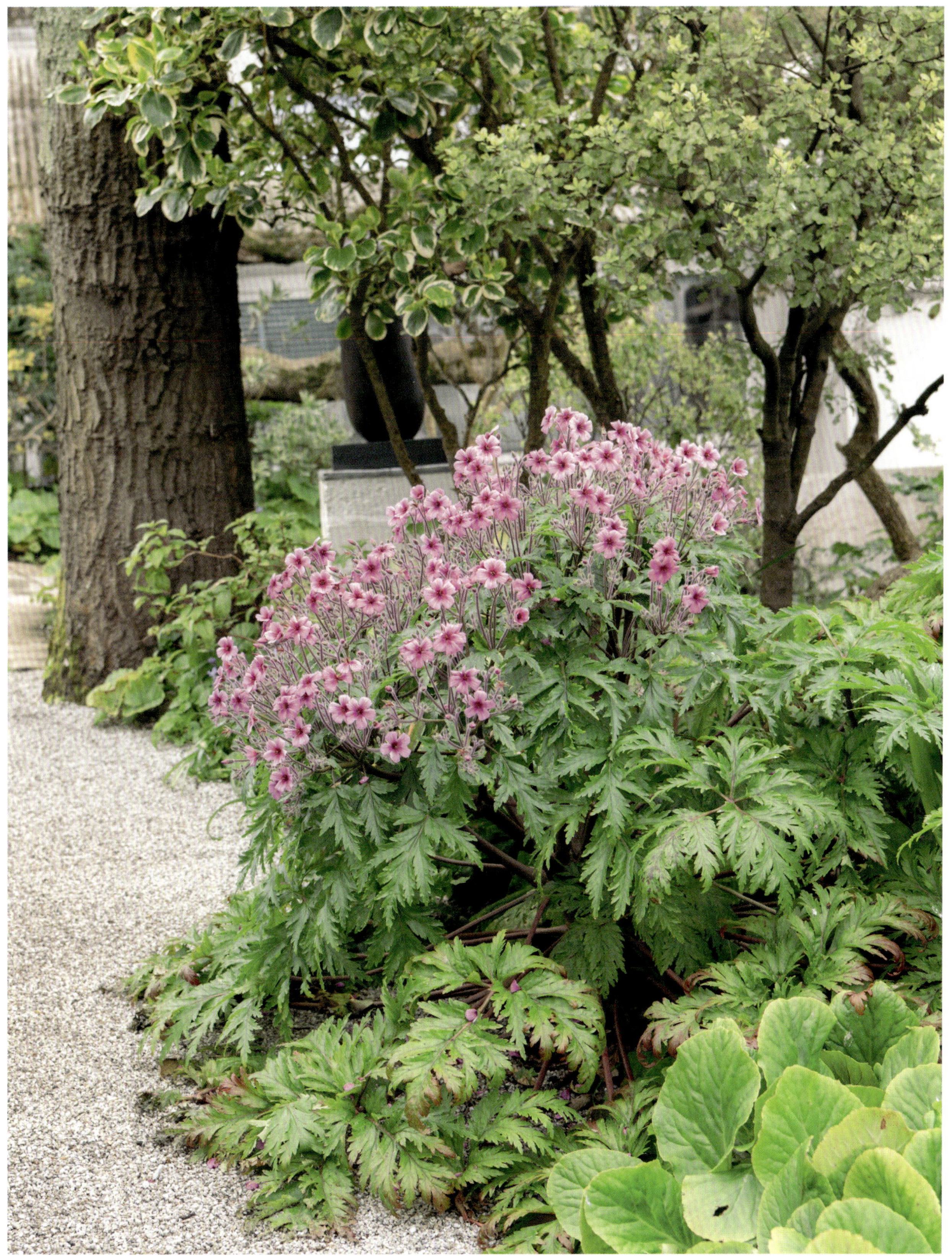

6 *Geranium maderense* giant herb robert, see also p.23

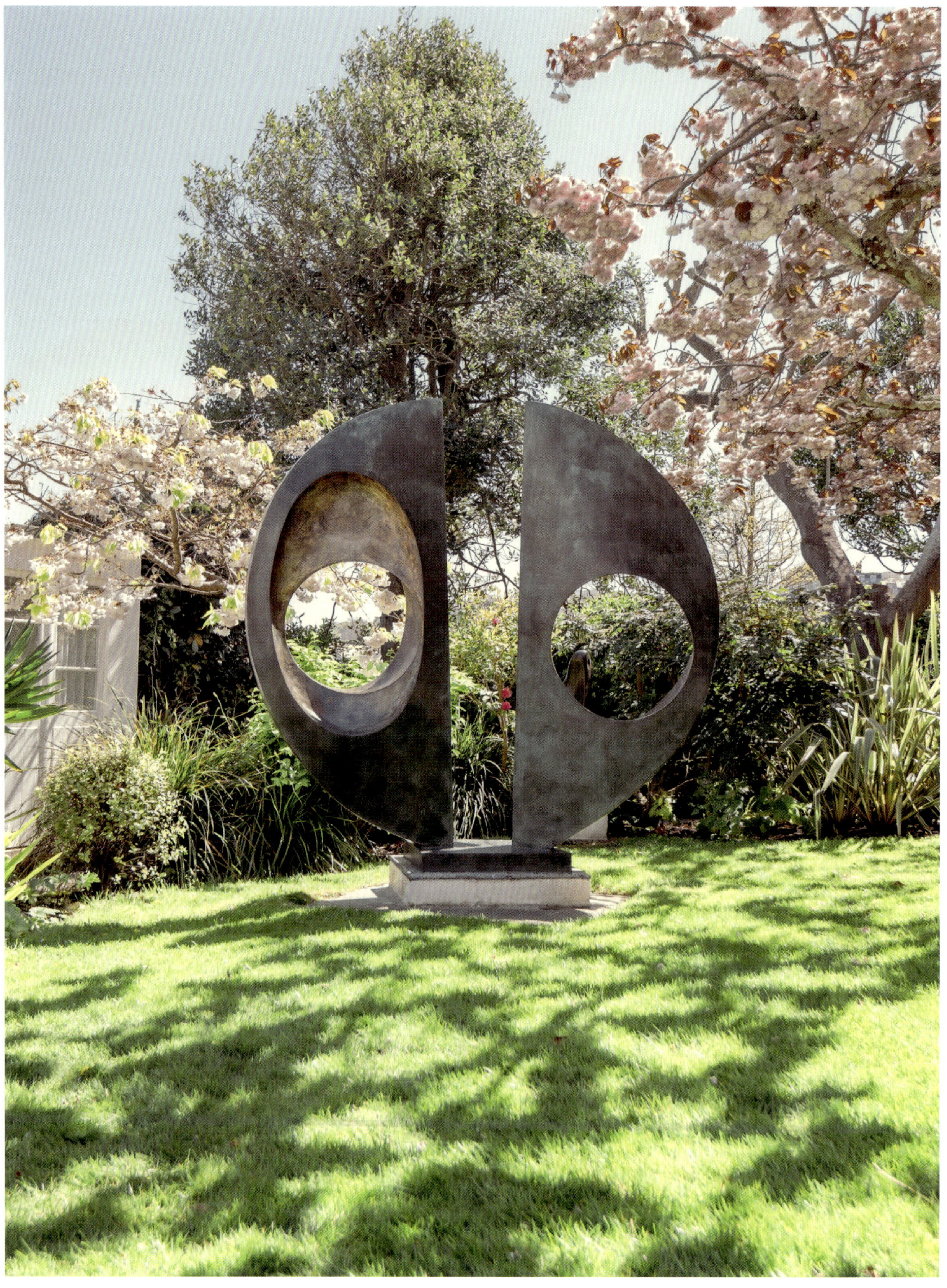

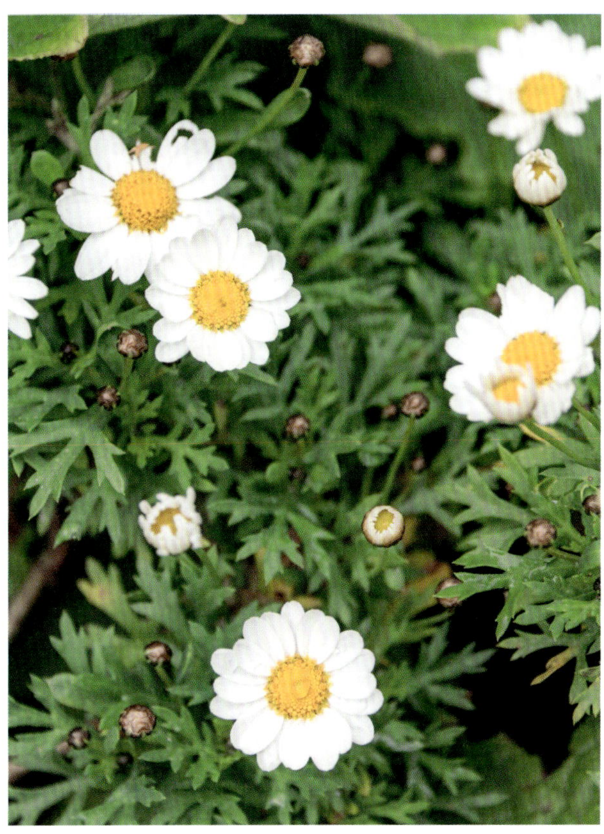

7 *Argyranthemum frutescens* marguerite

Two Forms (Divided Circle) 1969 (left)
These delicately poised forms have a dramatic quality: the viewer is both invited
to step through and denied access. Despite appearances, the sculpture is far
from symmetrical, with the shapes of the two elements and their holes being very
different. As in *Four-Square (Walk Through)*, the inside faces of the apertures were
originally highly polished and golden in colour. The sinuous edges of these
openings and the views they offer are important elements, introducing movement
and space to the composition.

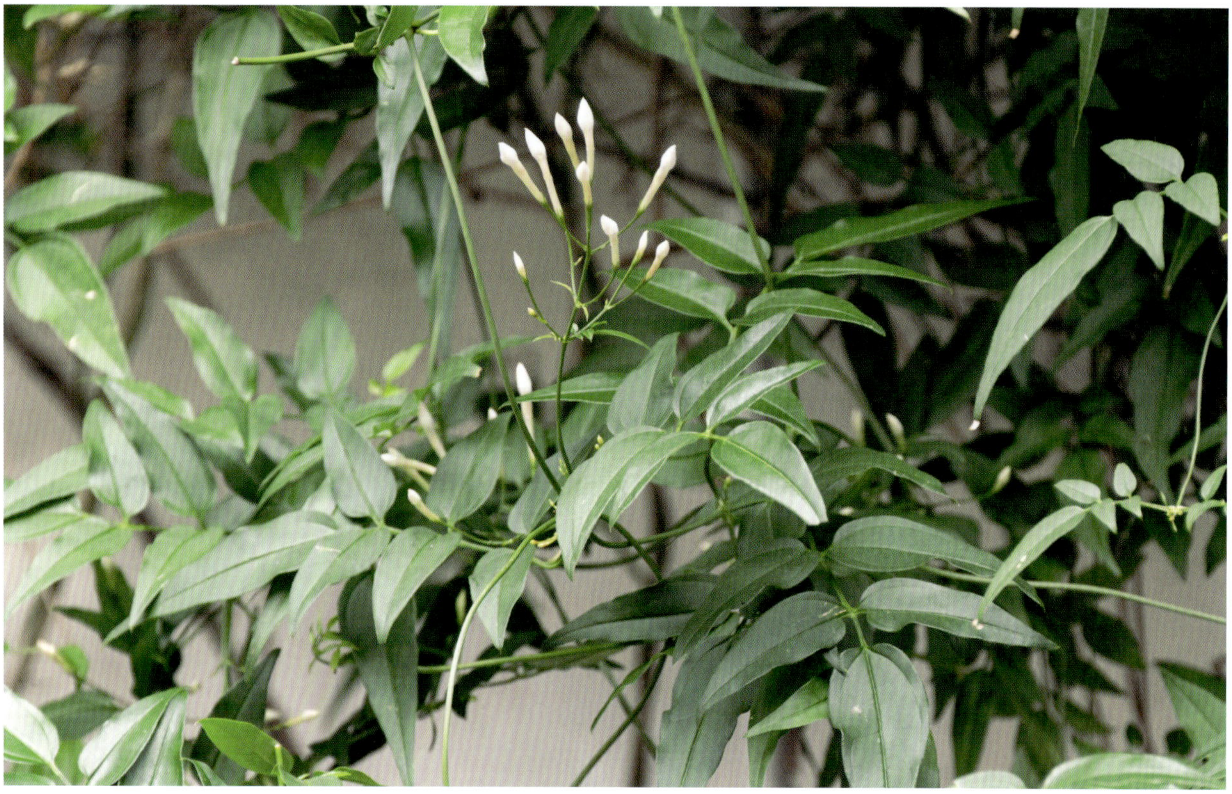

8   *Jasminum polyanthum* jasmine

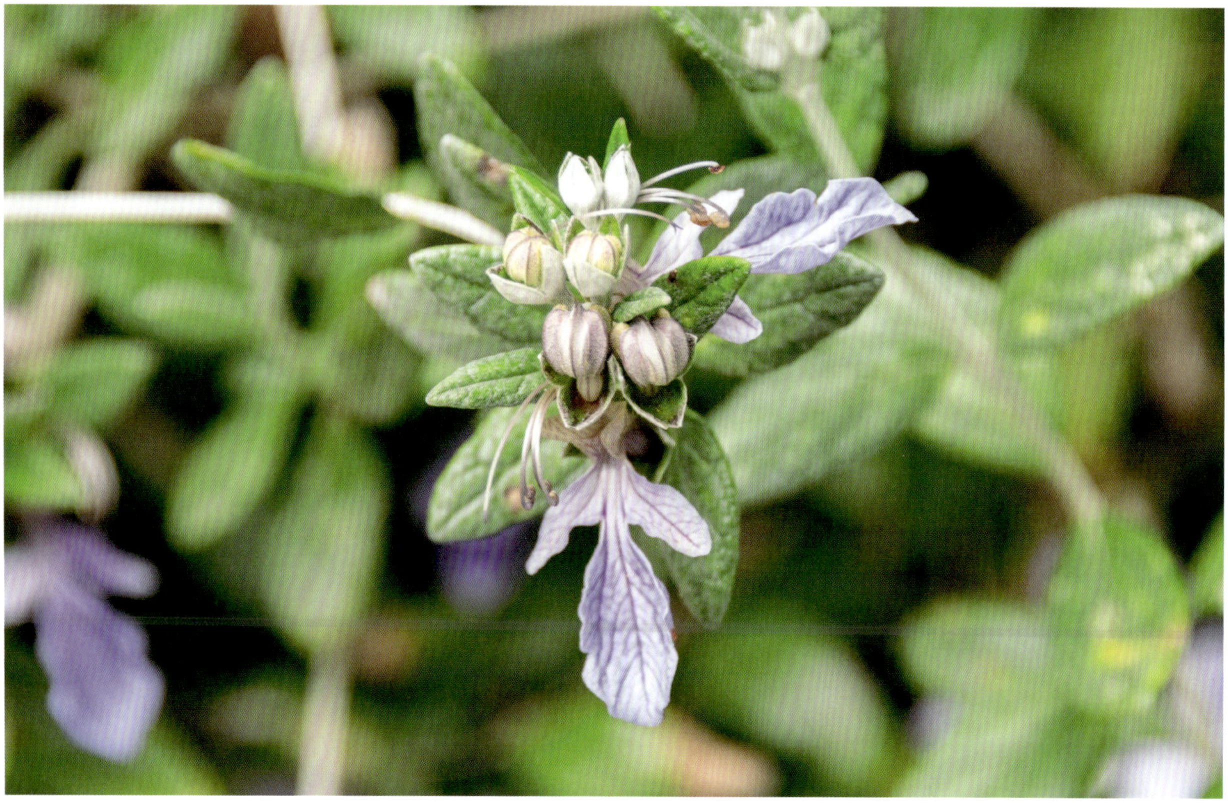

9   *Teucrium fruticans* tree germander

5   *Prunus* 'Accolade' cherry tree
The iconic and beautiful cherry tree, now in its latter years, is the most important plant to the garden. Although short-lived, the much-anticipated flowering of the cherry is celebrated by staff and visitors alike; an enchanting transformation for (usually) the last two weeks in May. The tree has grown wide but is prevented from growing too high by the Atlantic weather. Sculpted by oceanic winds, this distinct spreading form brings a unique and special character, adorning the garden with a ceiling of delicate pink when in flower. Lichen and moss form a living tapestry of greens through the upper branches but the deep copper red bark and horizontal lenticels that allow one to identify a cherry when it is not in leaf are still visible on the lower trunks. Creating a perfect partner with the blue-green patina of Hepworth's bronzes, the pendant, fully double blooms fade almost to white as they age, and then leave the lawn strewn with a confetti of shed petals.

6   *Geranium maderense* giant herb robert
The largest of the geranium species, *Geranium maderense* takes up to three years to reach flowering size. During this time, it produces large, glossy, deeply lobed, and toothed leaves, which are dark green and carried on stiff, red-tinted stems, radiating from a woody central stem. By the third year the plant should be mature enough to start its magnificent flowering spectacle; it begins when a spherical cluster of sticky-haired, pinkish-grey stems and buds form above the central rosette of leaves. The buds burst into a mass of rich, vibrant magenta flowers up to five feet high, and combine admirably with the cinerarias in the garden. The petals have a satin sheen, and their colour is the perfect counterpoint to the leaves. This plant enjoys the mild maritime climate and dappled shade of the museum garden. Although short-lived, and only flowering after three years, it comes with the highest commendation due to the large glossy, fern-like leaves and a show of flowers unrivalled by almost any other perennial, shade-tolerant plant.

7   *Argyranthemum frutescens* marguerite
This hardy, attractive subshrub is popular as a containerised plant, and is another of the museum garden plants that originates from the Canary Islands. Accordingly it is best suited to a well-drained soil and sunny position. A first-year marguerite will grow to one foot (thirty centimetres) or so and will produce many of its daisy-like white flowerheads from late April until September, aided by regular 'dead heading' of old blooms. The finely divided, fern-like leaves are evergreen, and, as the plant grows, the stems will take on a woody appearance. After four years the marguerite will, with care and pruning, be a bushy shape, and smothered in flowers all summer. It can reach a height of three feet (ninety centimetres) and may need support if it becomes top heavy.

8   *Jasminum polyanthum* jasmine
In March and April, the jasmine produces an abundance of star-shaped white flowers that fill the greenhouse with the unmistakable, heavenly fragrance that it is renowned for. White seemed to be a favourite flower colour of Hepworth's, running as a theme throughout the garden and seasons, and brings a timeless class and distinction to the planting. In the greenhouse this evergreen climber has year-round presence and structure with its dark glossy foliage. Originating from the mountains of southwest China, *Jasminum polyanthum* has great vigour and is easily grown in Hepworth's greenhouse. It is pest free and shade tolerant and will twine its way along and around anything it comes across, but is easily forgiven, being so sweetly scented.

9   *Teucrium fruticans* tree germander
Originating from the central and western Mediterranean countries, *Teucrium fruticans* is perfectly adapted to cope with our warming climate. It has white-felted shoots and green leaves, that appear silvery green due to lots of little hairs; their purpose is to reflect sunlight and protect the leaf. It is for this reason that silver leaved plants almost always demand full sun. *Teucrium* is a member of the mint family, and as such has the most intricately shaped little azure-blue flowers; however, you must be quite close to admire them. Outstandingly beautiful yet understated, it is a perfect plant for the Hepworth Garden, in that it does not fight for attention. The silver leaves provide gentle contrast with both the sculptures and surrounding planting. It is drought tolerant, a good coastal garden plant, and attracts a great number of bees so is sure to stand the test of time. The garden has an almost constant succession of flowers for various pollinators; in September often a hummingbird moth can be seen hovering and working methodically through the *Salvia microphylla*.

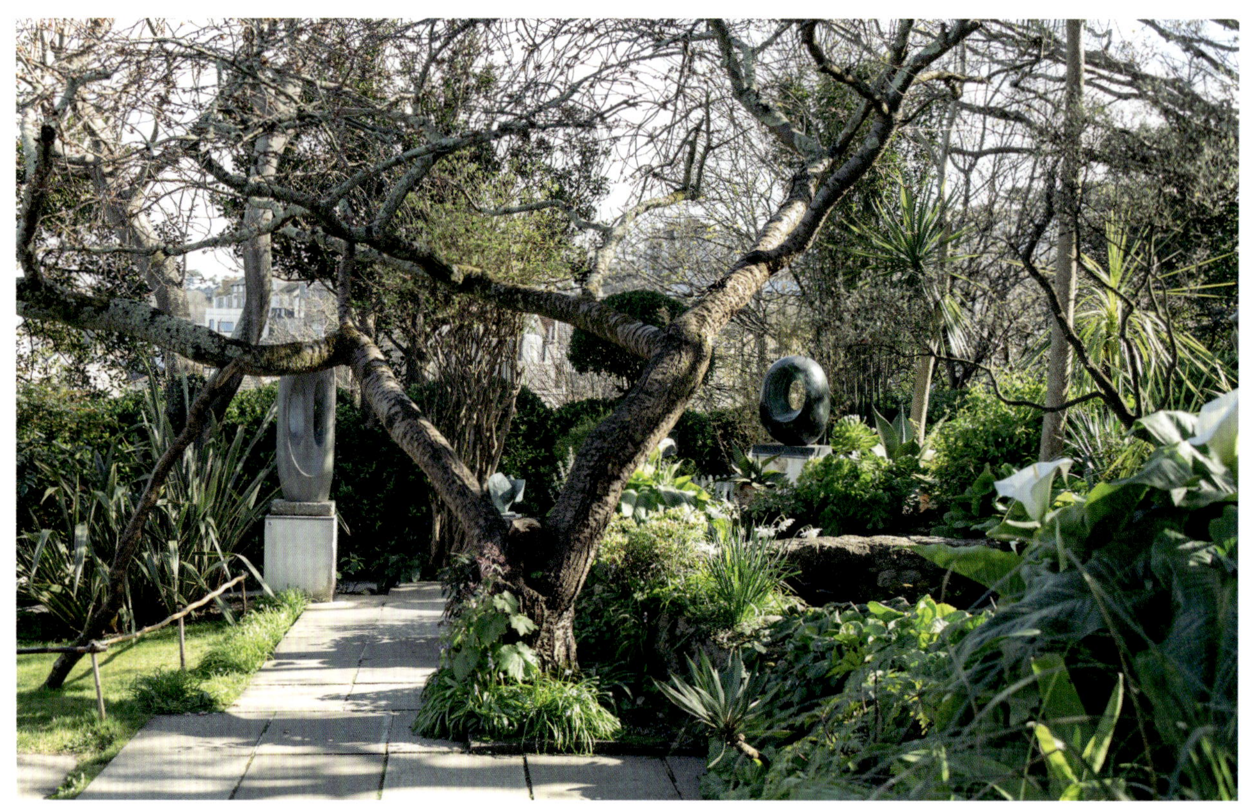

Cantate Domino 1958 (right)
The title of this work – 'O Sing unto the Lord' in Latin – is the opening line of Psalm 98, and reflects Hepworth's renewed spirituality following the death of her son, Paul, in 1953. While its form may suggest hands clasped in prayer, the rising movement of the composition seems celebratory. There is also the suggestion of organic growth, as the bronze appears to unfold out of the lower section like an emerging seedling. This combination of spirituality and nature is typical of the artist.

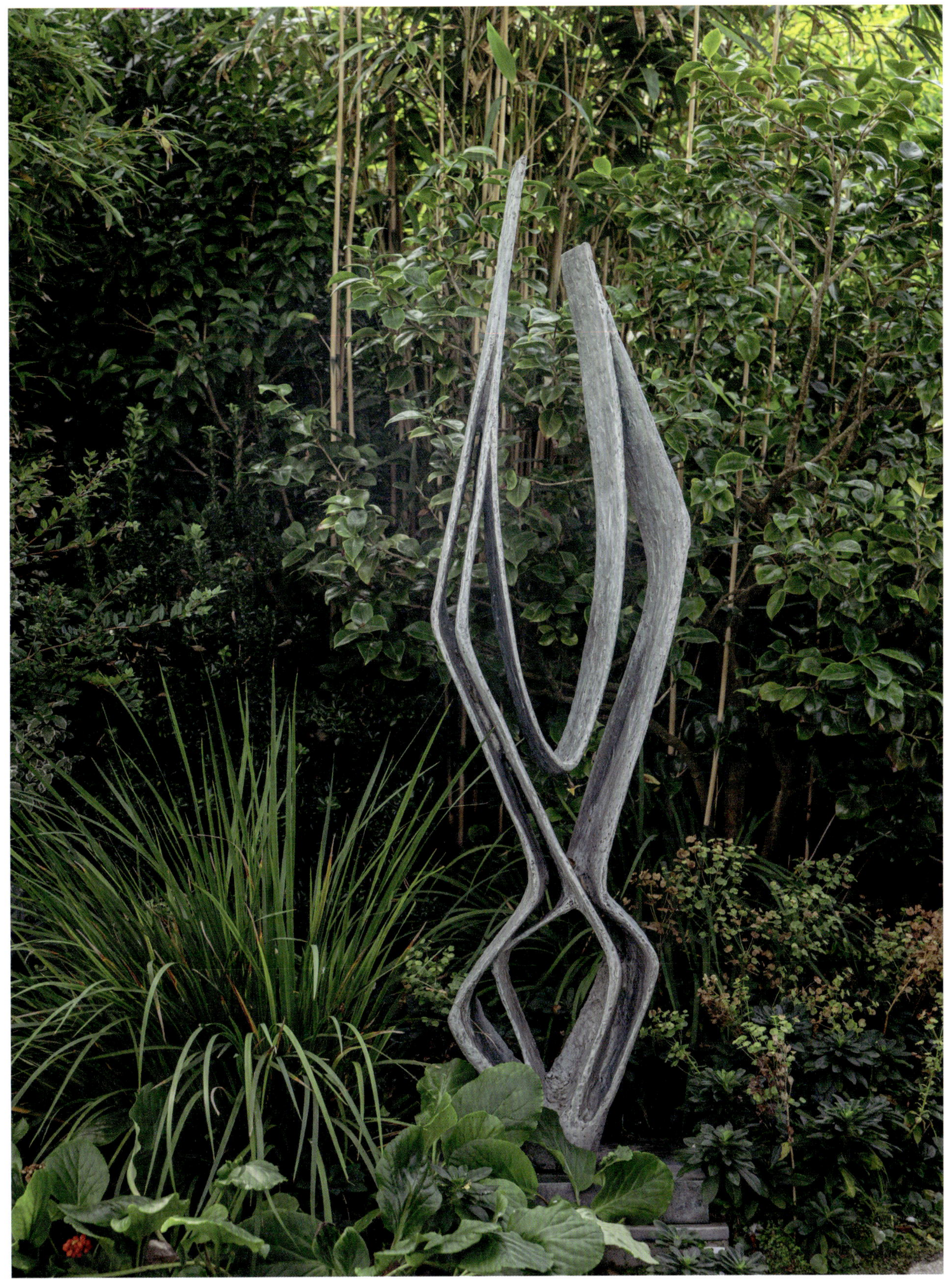

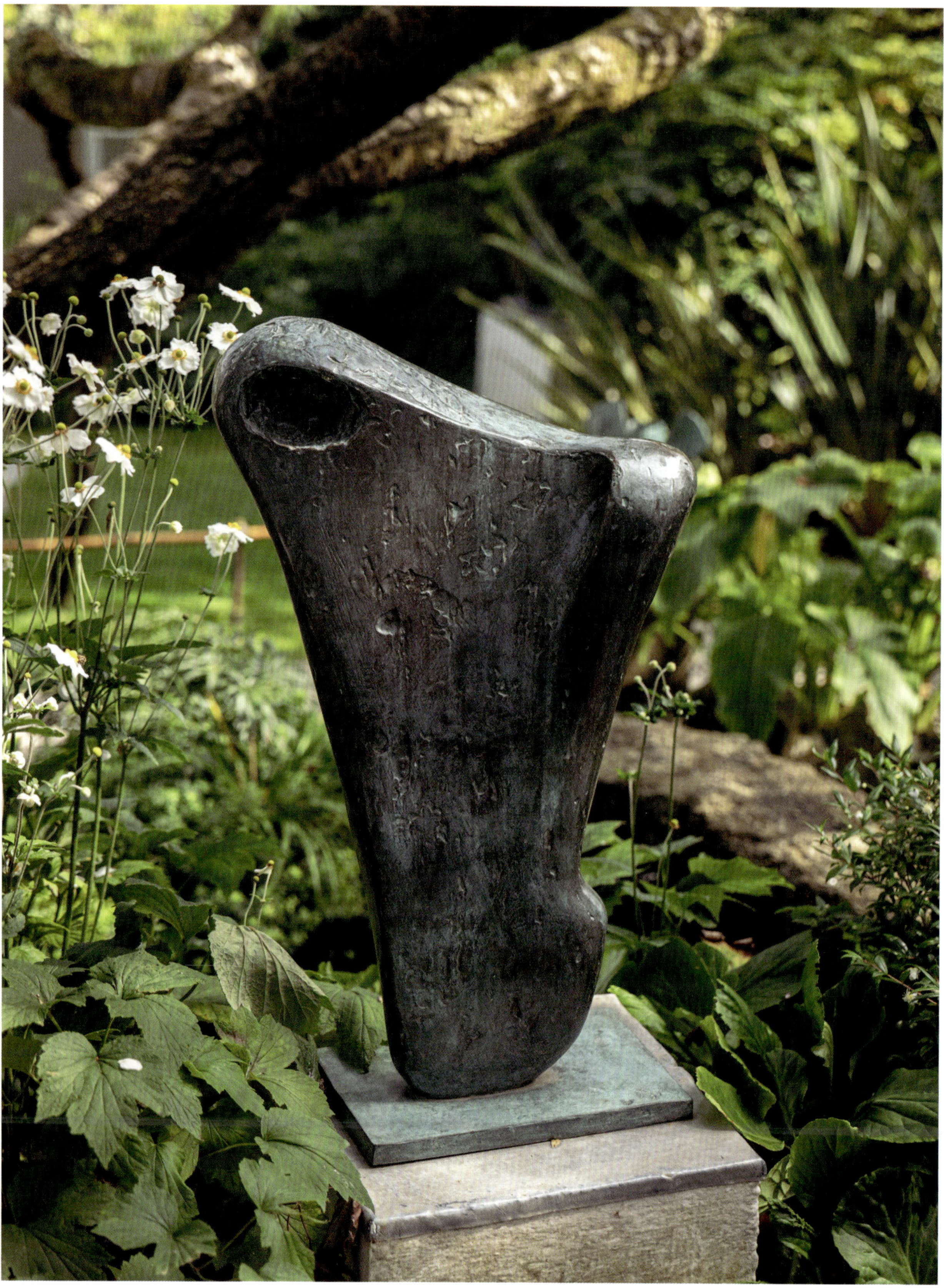

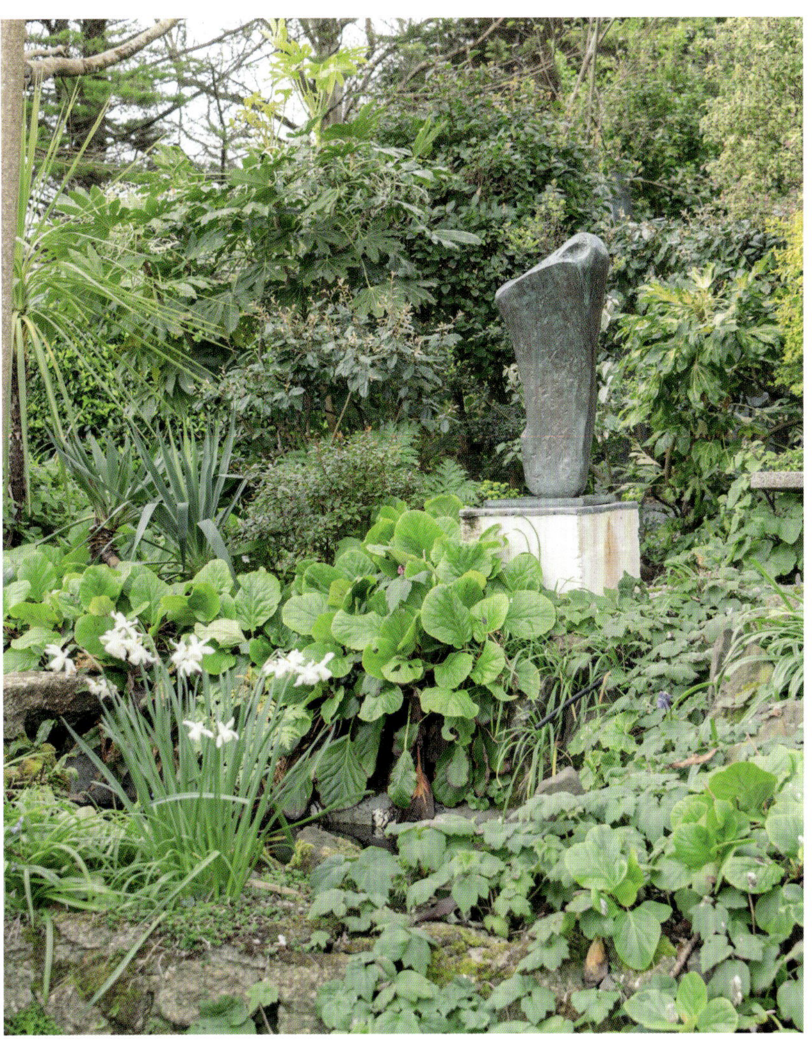

Torso II (Torcello) 1958 (left and above)
This is one of a series of three works suggesting both the human torso and
a single bone. Among Hepworth's most organic forms, these all have sub-titles
with marine or Mediterranean associations. Torcello is an island in the Venetian
lagoon that is renowned for its Byzantine basilicas and mosaics, which Hepworth
had visited. The artist photographed all three 'torsos' against the sea, and it may
be significant that she sited this piece in the garden close to water.

Summer

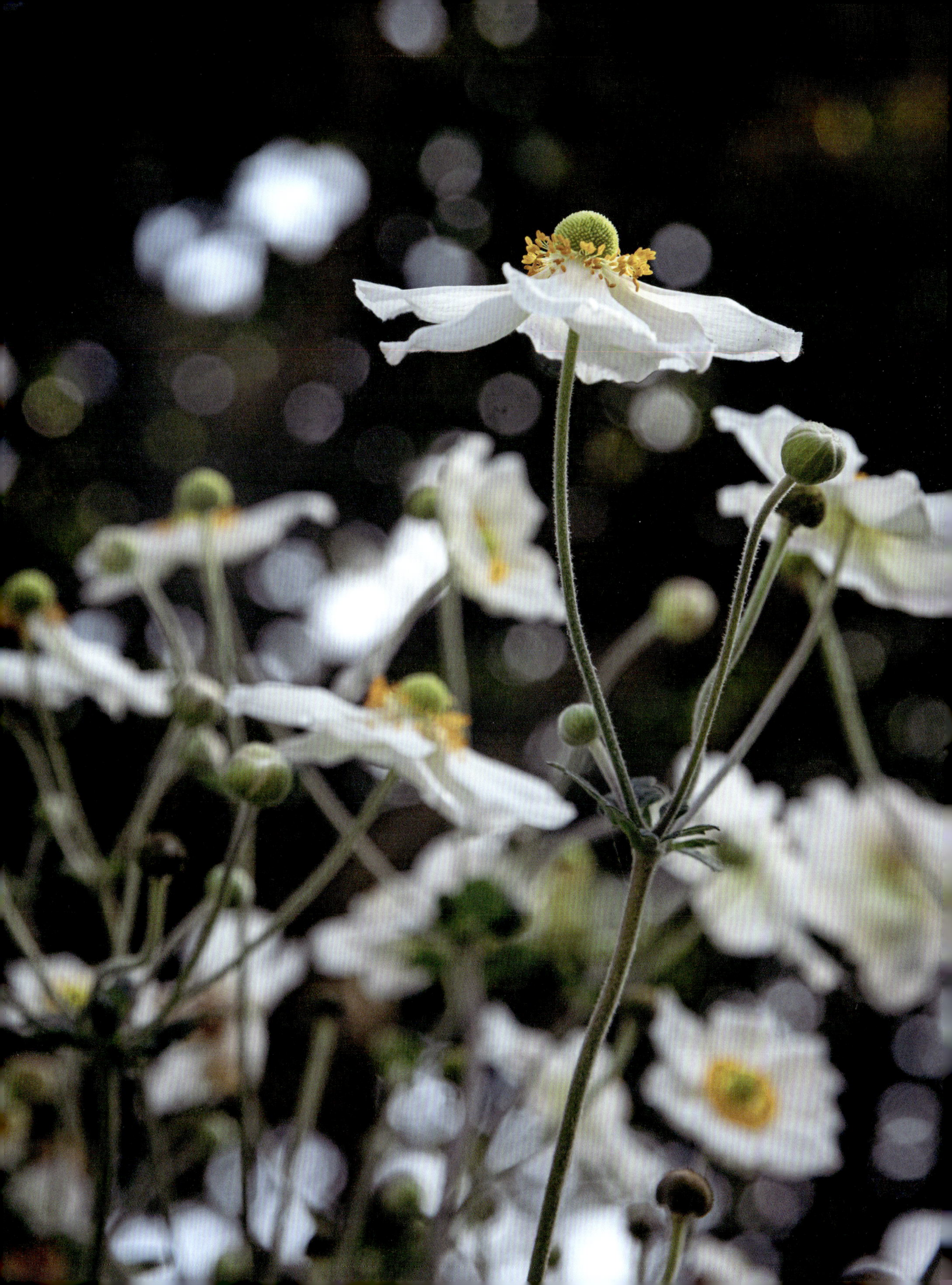

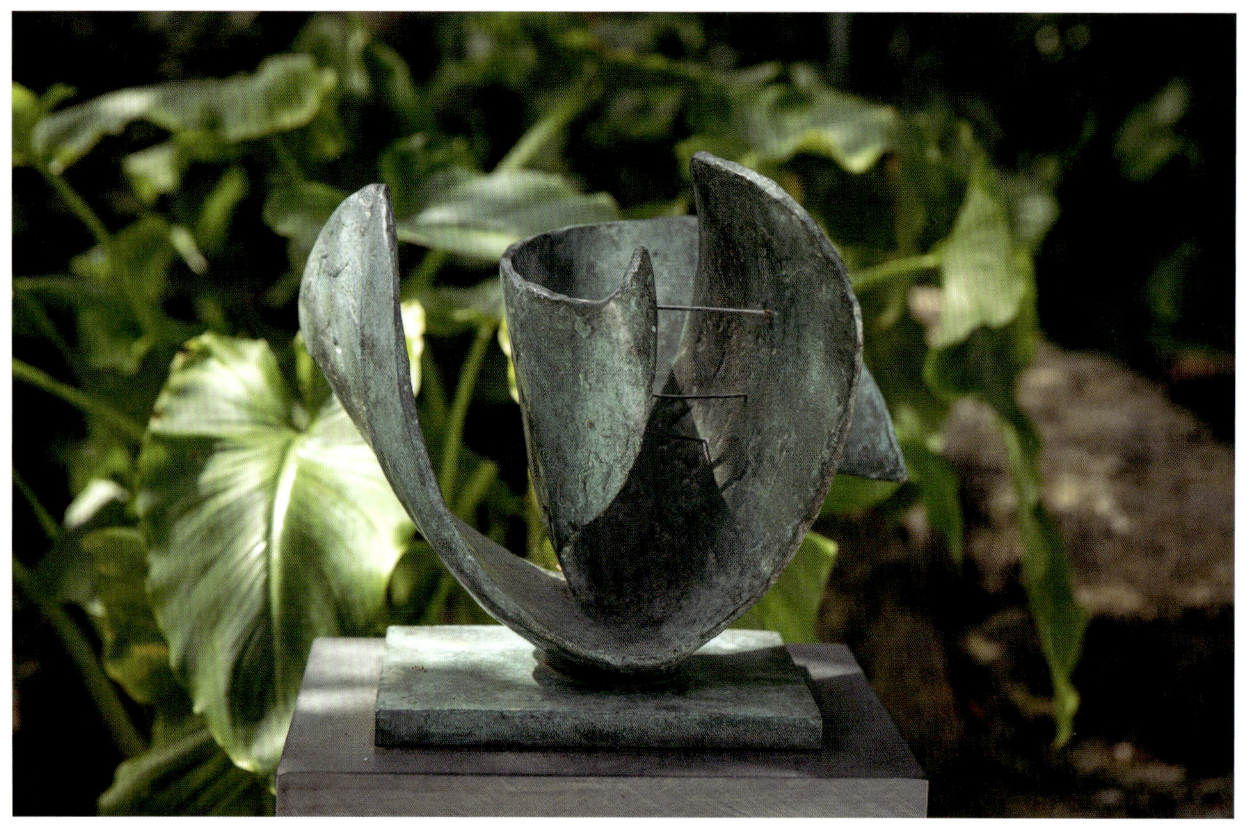

Corymb 1959 (above)
Hepworth's use of nature as a source for her art is especially clear in this work. A corymb is a floral cluster in which the buds are borne on long stems that rise from a single, unbranched stalk, giving a flat head of flowers. As the sculpture is not consistent with that definition, it seems likely that Hepworth wished simply to conjure up a general idea of inflorescence. Her positioning of the work amongst the flowers and foliage of the garden reinforces the association.

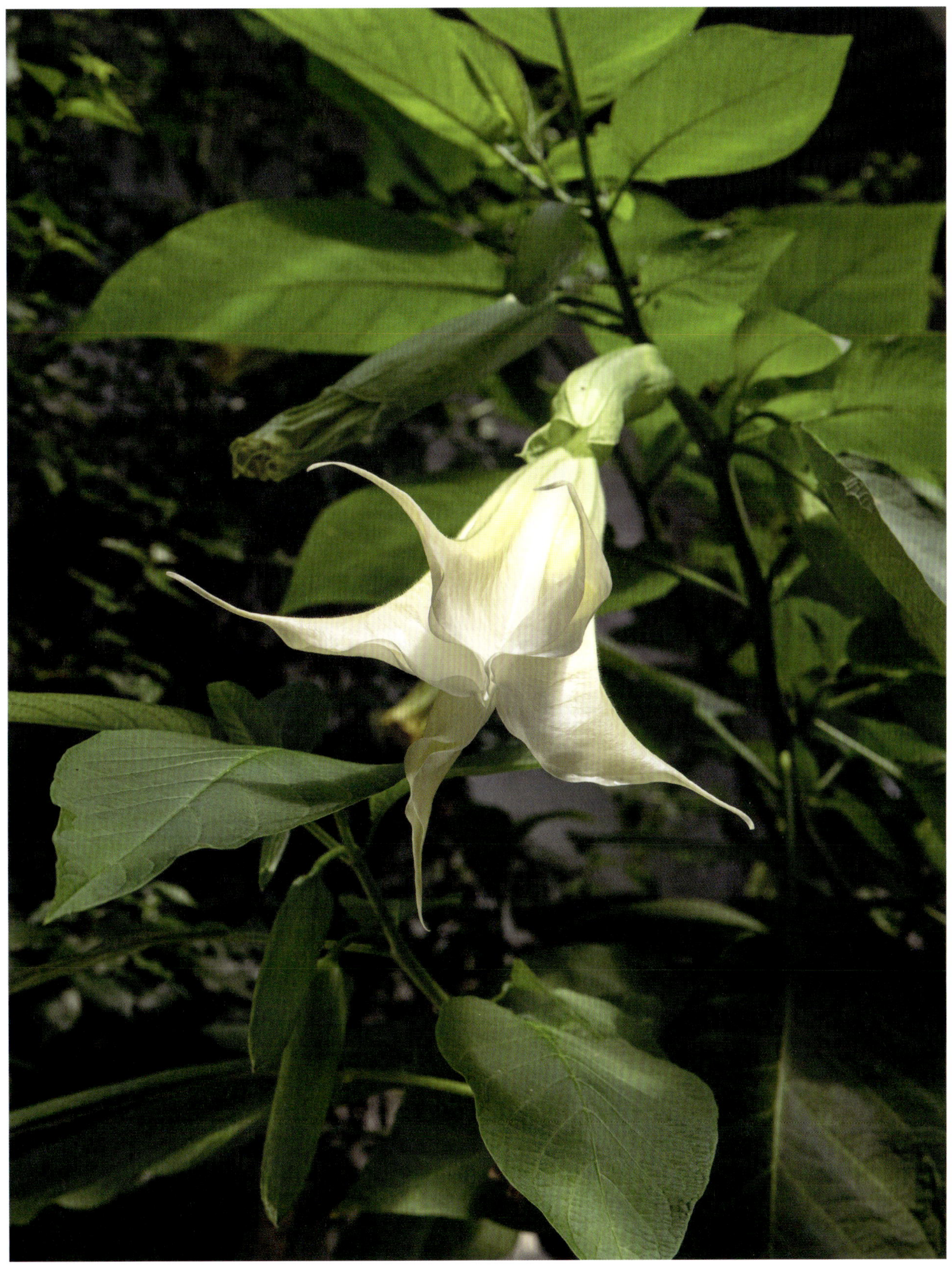

10 *Brugmansia suaveolens* angel's trumpets

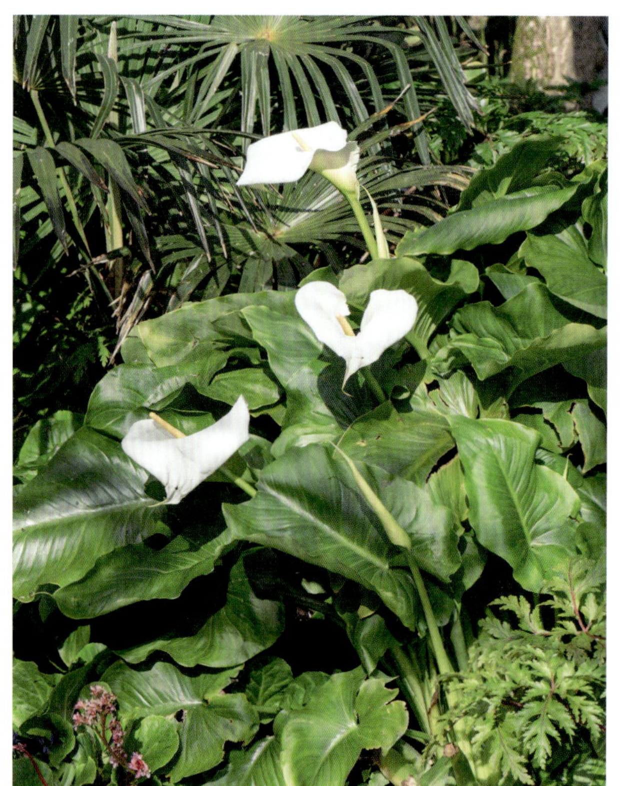 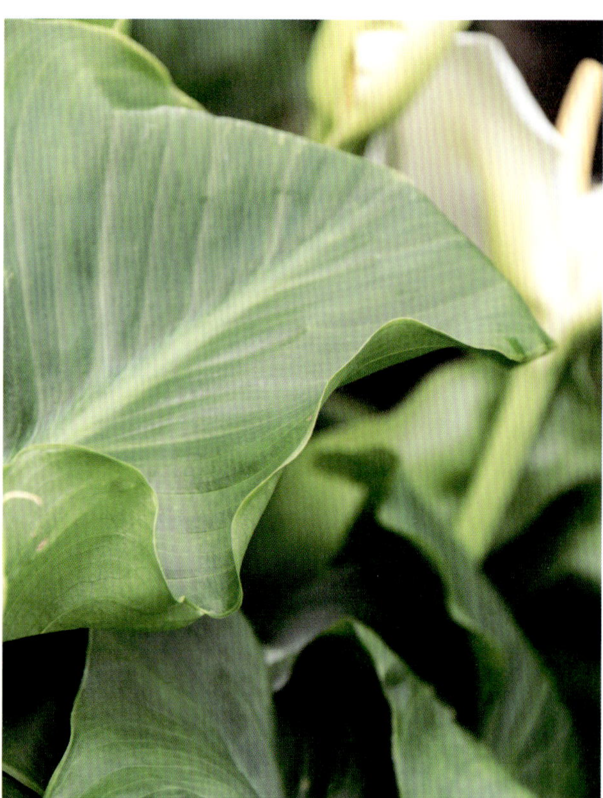

11 *Zantedeschia aethiopica* 'Crowborough' arum lily 'Crowborough'

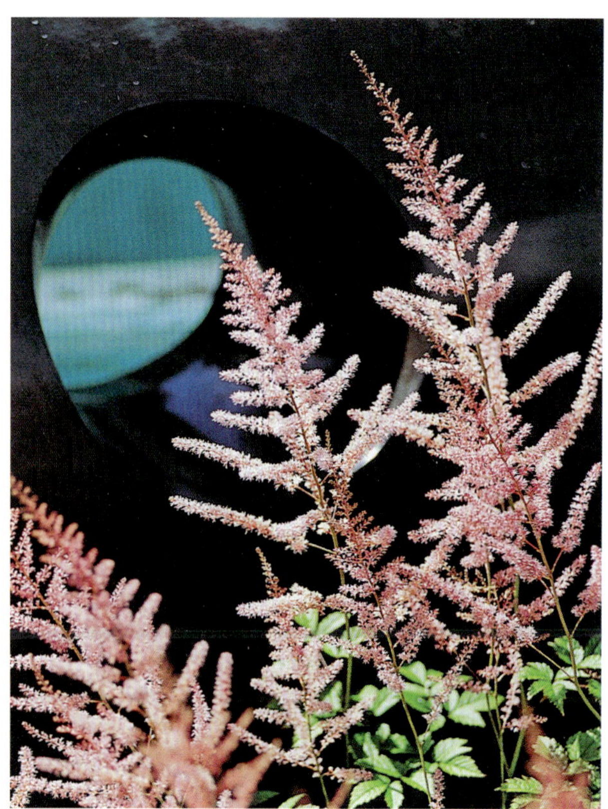

12 *Astilbe* astilbe

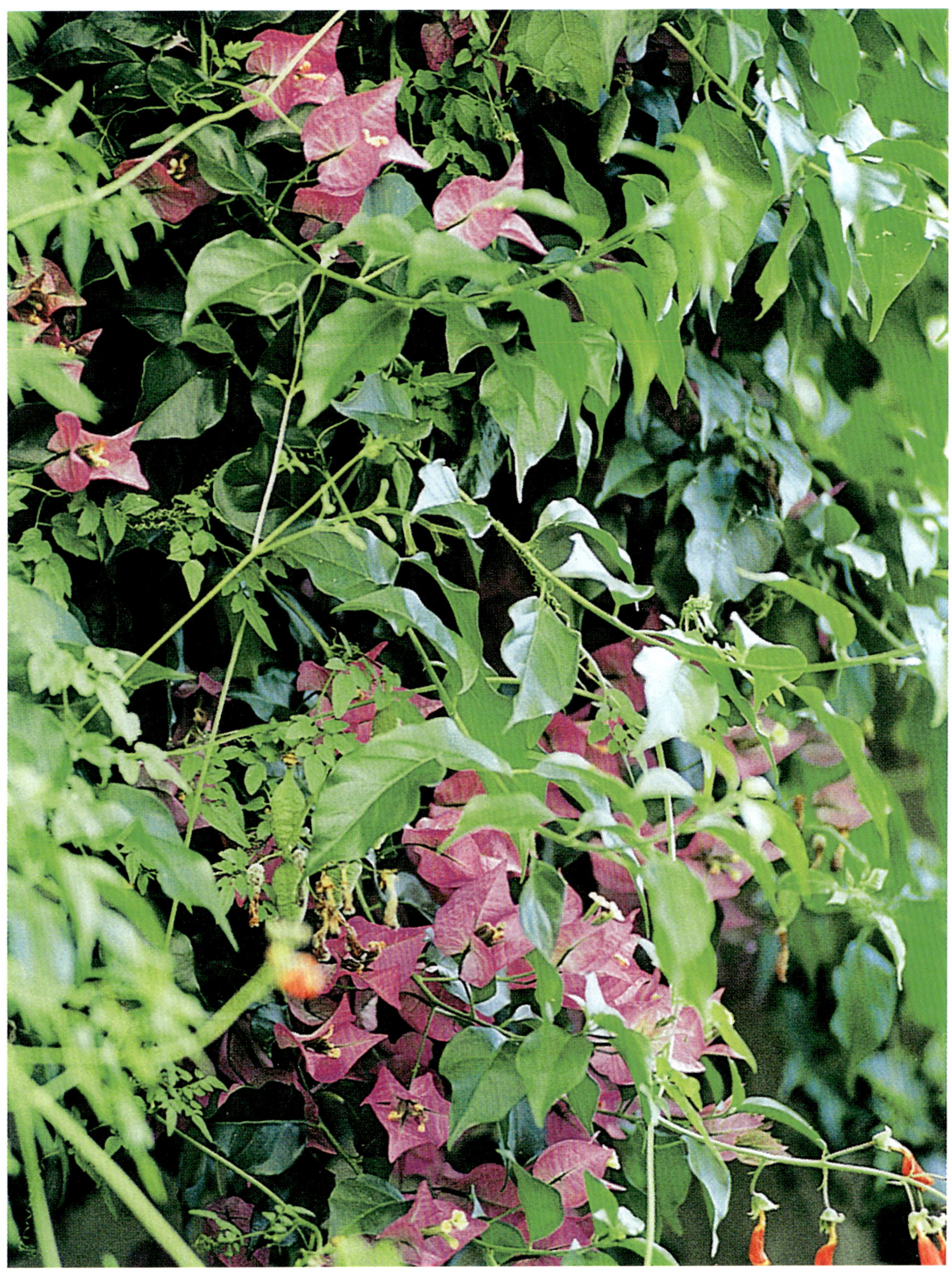

13 *Bougainvillea glabra* paper flower

10   *Brugmansia suaveolens* angel's trumpets
Sometimes referred to by an older name, *Datura*, *Brugmansia* is originally from South America. In the UK it is a tender plant, needing winter protection, so it is grown in the greenhouse. Now extinct in the wild, it only exists as a cultivated plant, but a rather special one at that. It adds the most exotic ambience to the greenhouse with its large, pendulous, trumpet-shaped white flowers, which can grow to thirty centimetres long. It is pollinated by nocturnal moths, and for this reason the *Brugmansia suaveolens* is night scented; this is often the case for white flowered plants, the bright inflorescences also acting as a guiding light for the moths at night. It flowers prolifically from mid-summer to late autumn, with heavy feeding, and as such it is much admired and commented on. A word of warning though: it is a member of the nightshade family and is highly poisonous if ingested.

11   *Zantedeschia aethiopica* 'Crowborough'
     arum lily 'Crowborough'
This dramatic, easy to grow and rewarding perennial tolerates most soils, but loves water and grows very well as a marginal pond plant. Originally from South Africa, it is hardy, usually evergreen in mild areas such as Cornwall and provides beautiful bold architectural foliage throughout the year. Arrowhead-shaped, rich green leaves grow to about twenty-five centimetres long and to a height of about sixty centimetres. Later, rising above these leaves, are borne showy pure-white hood flowers that unfurl in an echo of the fluid movement of the sculpture *Corymb* 1959 so close to them. This is achieved with only one 'petal', which is botanically a bract that swirls around the true flower inside.

12   *Astilbe* astilbe
A member of the saxifrage family, astilbes can vary from twenty to one hundred and twenty centimetres high, in shades from white through to pinks and deep carmine. They have broad leaves divided into oval, deeply toothed leaflets, which are usually dark green but sometimes flushed with bronze. Elegant, feathery panicles of tiny star-shaped blooms are carried well above the foliage on slender stems, and are attractive to bees, butterflies and other pollinating insects. Occasionally known as Prince of Wales' feathers, astilbes prefer moist, partly shaded sites, but can perform well in drier, sunnier spots and benefit from an annual spring mulch of well-rotted compost. They can be propagated by careful division in spring or autumn, or grown from ripened seed. It is a perennial plant that dies back in the winter; as with many perennials, it is best not to cut the dried flower spikes down until March, as they provide good winter interest until then.

13   *Bougainvillea glabra* paper flower
Bougainvilleas, named after the scientist and explorer Louis de Bougainville, are tender climbers. *Bougainvillea glabra* is a semi-evergreen that retains most of its dark-green, oval leaves in temperatures above ten degrees Celsius. Although too tender to grow outdoors, bougainvilleas flourish even in cold greenhouses, rapidly reaching heights of six metres and a similar spread, requiring a trellis in their second or third year of growth. They like fertile, well-drained soil and a lot of light – the more sun the plant gets, the more brilliant its showy magenta 'flowers'. These are really floral bracts, like those of a poinsettia, but provide a colourful background for the true bloom – a tiny cream structure. The bracts, which look as delicate as tissue paper, are borne throughout the summer and well into autumn. There are many other species with vibrant colours available – reds, yellows, pinks and purples – though they are not easy to find and most of them need higher temperatures than *B. glabra*.

14   *Fuchsia magellanica* fuchsia
Named after the German physician and herbalist Leonard Fuchs (1506–66), the fuchsia was originally a southern-hemisphere plant that has been extensively developed since its introduction to Britain in 1800. The hardiest form, *F. magellanica*, is easily propagated, very wind tolerant, and forms attractive hedges, especially if regularly cut back hard. They are very bee-friendly plants. A fuchsia hedge will filter the wind more effectively than a solid windbreak, helping to prevent turbulence inside the garden. It has small dark-green leaves, which are reddish when young, and it is strung with pairs of garnet and purple flowers from April to November. Prune fuchsias in March or April all the way to the ground, if desired, for the best results. Hybrid fuchsias are generally less hardy but come in an ever-increasing variety of flower types and colours, many resembling icing-sugar decorations.

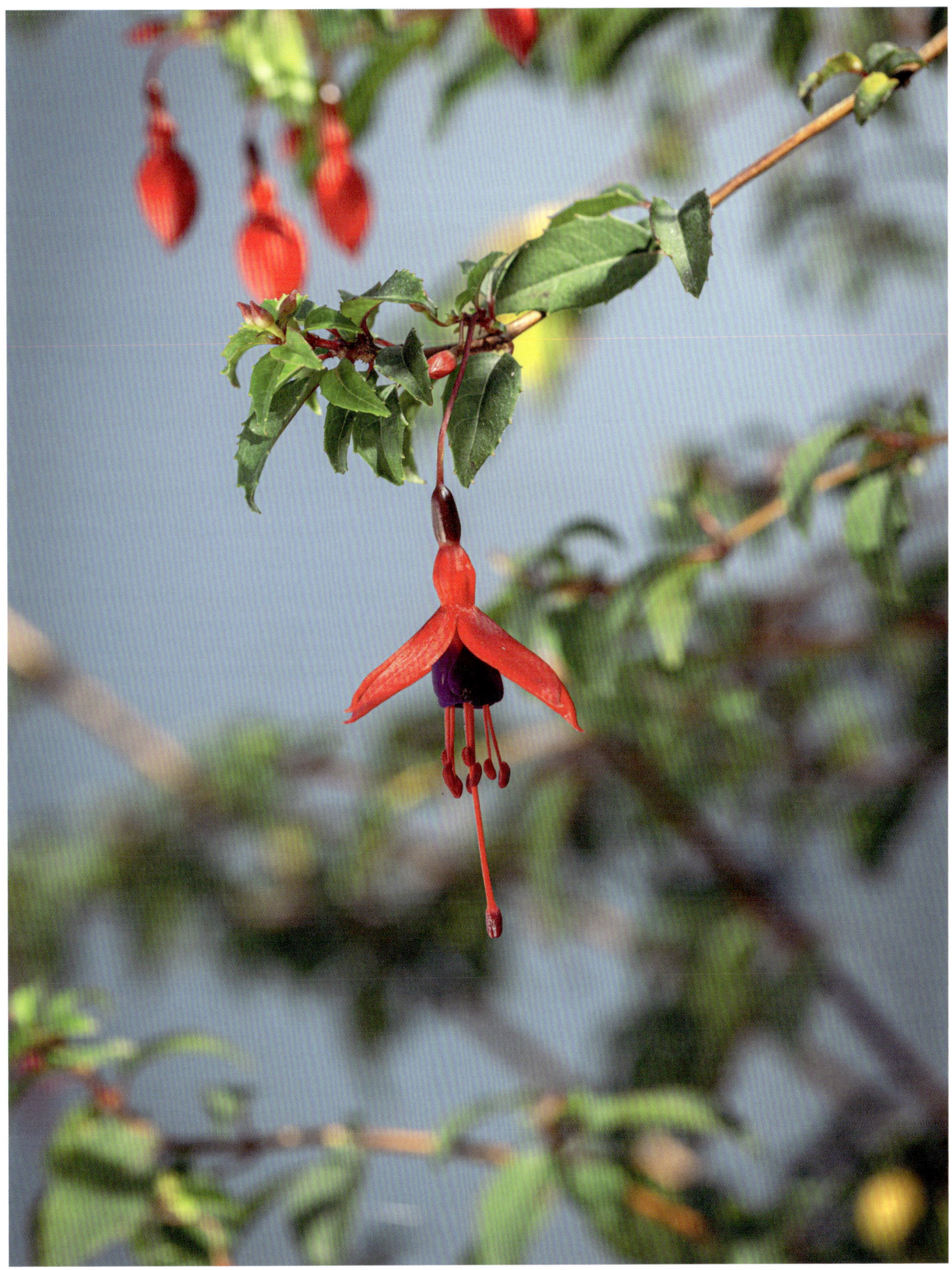

14 *Fuchsia magellanica* fuchsia

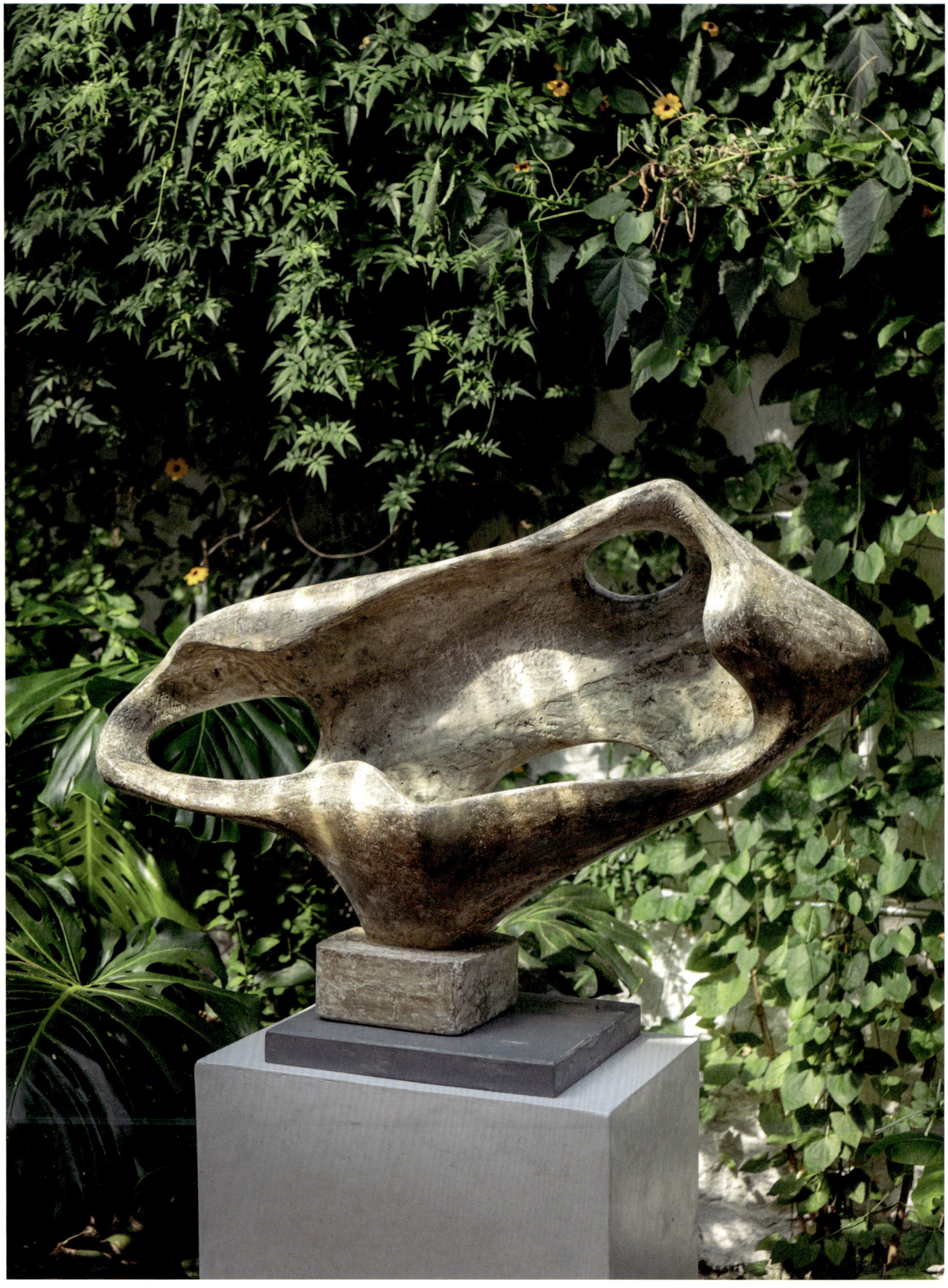

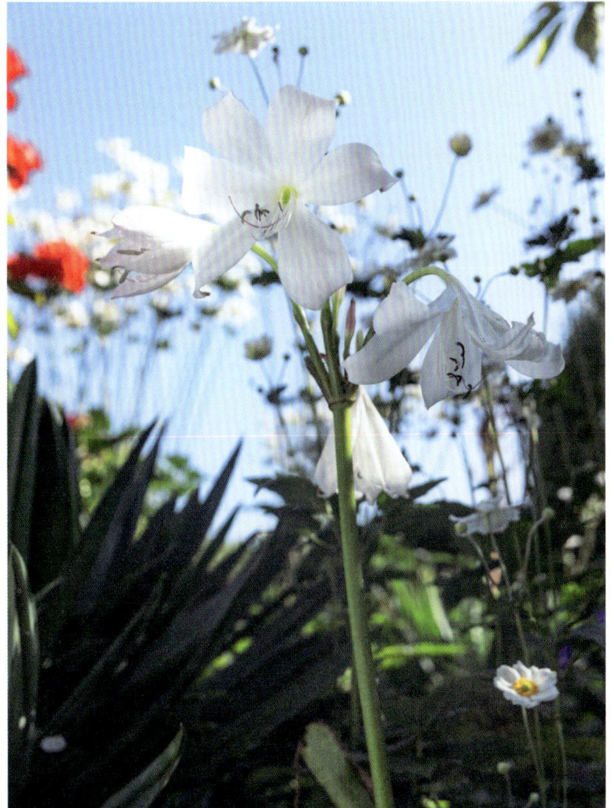 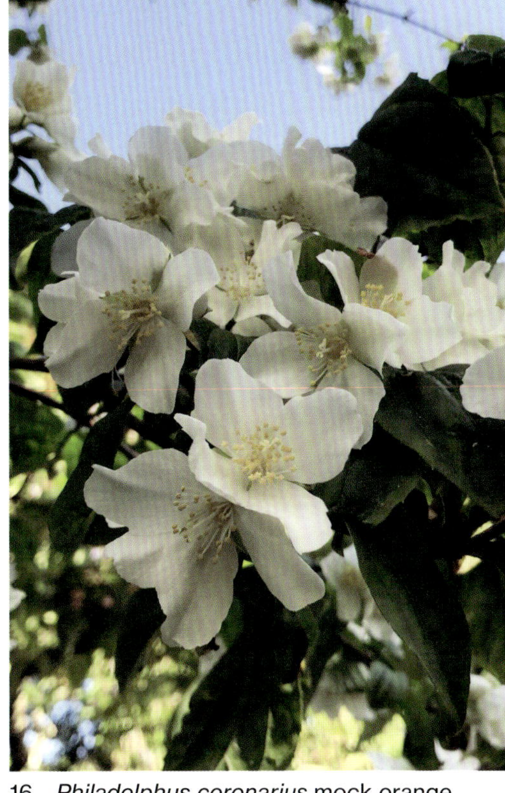

15 *Crinum x powelli* 'Album' white Powell lily   16 *Philadelphus coronarius* mock orange

Sea Form (Porthmeor) 1958 (left)
This is the plaster from which an edition of seven bronzes was cast. It may have been painted this bronze-like colour when exhibited in St Ives Guildhall in 1968. The title refers to a nearby beach, known for its long waves rolling in from the Atlantic. While the curled edges of the sculpture echo the form of a turning wave, the patination seems to emulate the colour of the sea. More generally, the sculpture's irregularity, expansive form and ambiguous space recreate aspects of the natural realm.

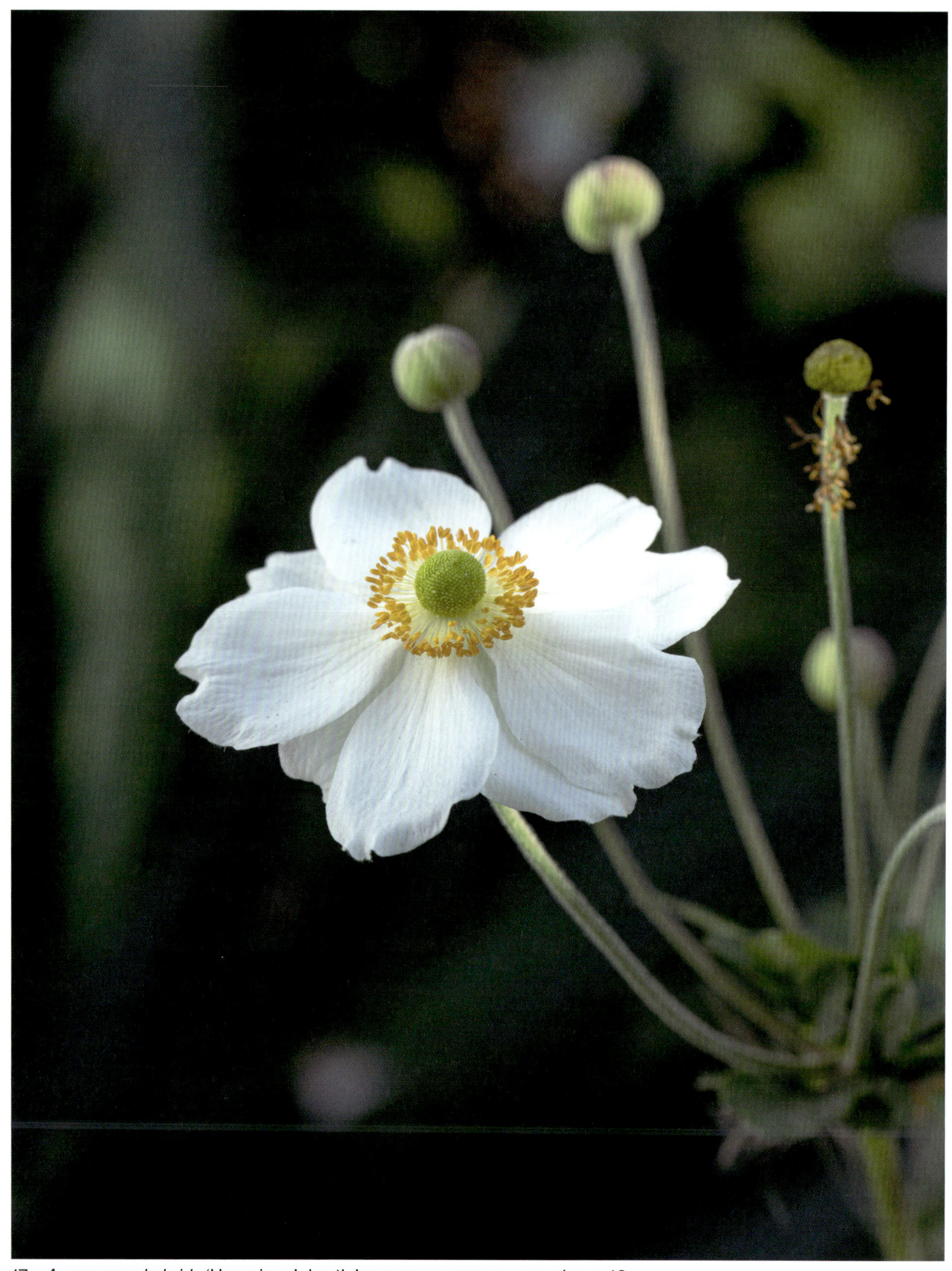

17   *Anemone x hybrida* 'Honorine Jobert' Japanese anemone, see also p.43

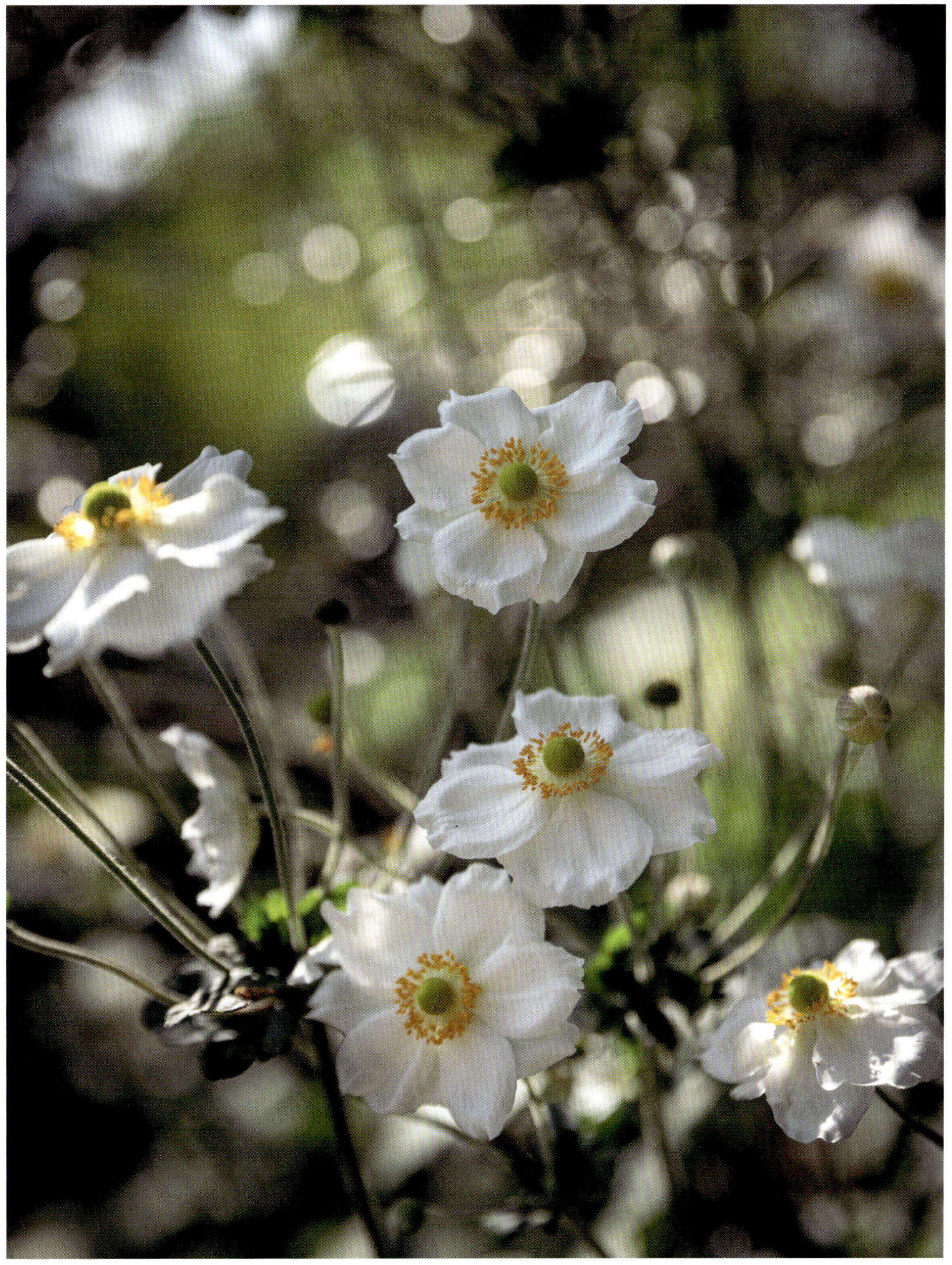

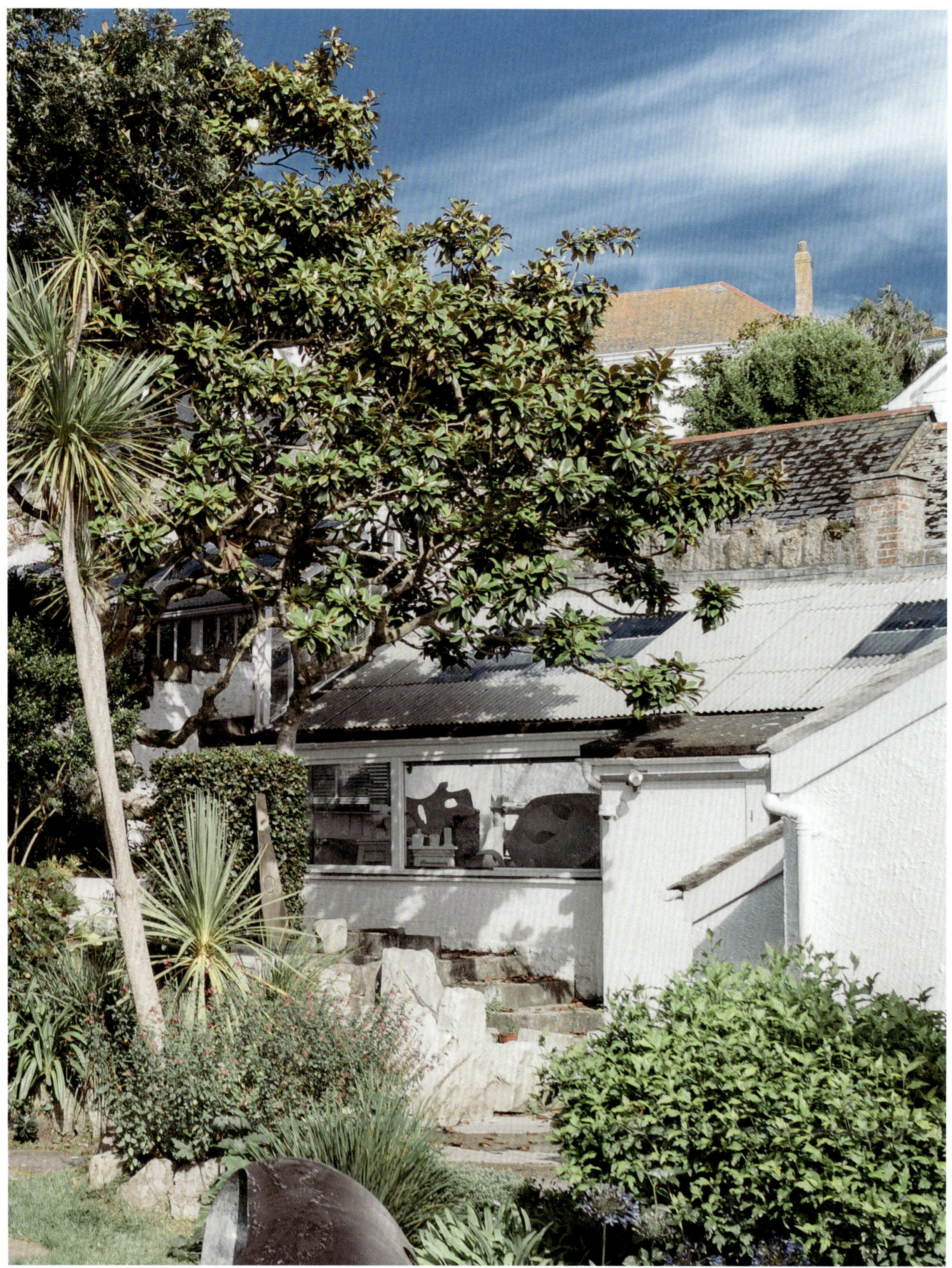

18 *Magnolia grandiflora* bull bay

15   *Crinum x powellii* 'Album' white Powell lily
This beautiful, fragrant, clump-forming perennial is a
hybrid from two crinums that both originate from South
Africa; one, *C. bulbispermum* from along the banks of
streams and the other, *C. moorei*, from forests. Where
a plant originates from gives strong indication of its
preferred growing conditions and accordingly, *Crinum
x powellii* enjoys a moist, humus-rich soil and light
dappled shade. Growing from perhaps one hundred, to
one hundred and twenty centimetres tall, this member
of the amaryllis family makes an elegant, delicate
and tropical addition to the museum garden with its
six-pointed, star-shaped pure-white flowers. The foliage
is exuberant, exotic and lush, and makes a tasty treat
for a snail. However, a layer of wool pellets serves as
a nature-friendly and effective barrier against these
pesky pests. Keep out of midday sun to avoid scorching
the large, strappy, arching leaves and give it a good
mulch in the winter.

16   *Philadelphus coronarius* mock orange
This deciduous shrub originates from south-east
Europe where it populates rocky outcrops and screes.
In the UK it has been cultivated since around the
sixteenth century, remaining popular due to the profuse
and sweetly scented flowers that appear in racemes of
five to nine blossoms. The species epithet *coronarius*
means used for garlands, giving a clue to historic
usage. The *Philadelphus* in the museum garden is
certainly of unique form; the twisted and gnarly woody
stems to two and a half metres are cleared of new
growth. Flowering stems grow from the very top of this
quirky and much-admired structure, blooming and filling
the air with their delightful fragrance. *Philadelphus*
should never be 'blobbed', that is cut or topiarised like a
hedge, instead cut out the oldest third of stems to
ground level immediately after flowering. In the museum
garden, ground level is considered to be eight-foot high
so the characterful woody framework can remain.

17   *Anemone x hybrida* 'Honorine Jobert'
      Japanese anemone
Traditionally associated with Japanese gardens,
hence the name, *Anemone* x *hybrida* is actually a cross
between two Chinese species, *A. huphensis* and *A.
vitifolia*. This particular cultivar, 'Honorine Jobert', was
first discovered in Verdun, France in 1858. It has now
long been a favourite in the UK, requiring little care to
produce bright single blooms that are a welcome arrival
to borders through late summer and into autumn, when
most other flowers have been and gone. Borne on stems
to just over one metre high that wave gracefully in the
breeze, each flower contains a cluster of sunshine
yellow stamens, framed by pure white petals. In
addition, they are very attractive to bees. The leaves
are palmate, toothed, and dark green. A member of the
buttercup family, it slowly spreads, and can over-run

other perennials. 'Honorine Jobert' is best suited to a
woodland environment, and perhaps even a bed all to
itself, where the bright white flowers can brighten up a
shady area.

18   *Magnolia grandiflora* bull bay
First introduced to Europe in 1711, this southern USA
species can grow between eighteen and twenty-four
metres high. It is one of the most primitive flowering
plants and the blooms are evocative of ancient times;
simple, large, bowl-shaped cream-white flowers up
to twenty-five centimetres across are produced
sporadically throughout the summer and early autumn.
It is the heat of these warmer months that prompts the
tree to bloom and the hotter it is, the more it will flower.
Of exquisite beauty and sweetly scented, once finished,
the petals fall, and what was once a flower becomes a
reddish-brown fruit that looks like a textured cone. Shiny,
waxy, deep green foliage, with a rust colour on the
underneath side, adorns the branches and being one
of very few evergreen trees in the museum garden, it is
highly valued. Planted by Barbara Hepworth, it is now of
great stature and semi-mature at around sixty years
old. However, like all the large trees in the museum
garden, it is kept lower than it might otherwise be by
Atlantic winds. Along with the copper beech, oak,
gingko and pear, it is lightly crown-thinned when
required to allow important filtered and dappled light
through to the sculptures, planting and greenhouse
below. This dappled light is an important and magical
feature of the museum garden that, combined with
wind and the moving sun, manifests in ever-changing
dancing shadows throughout the garden.

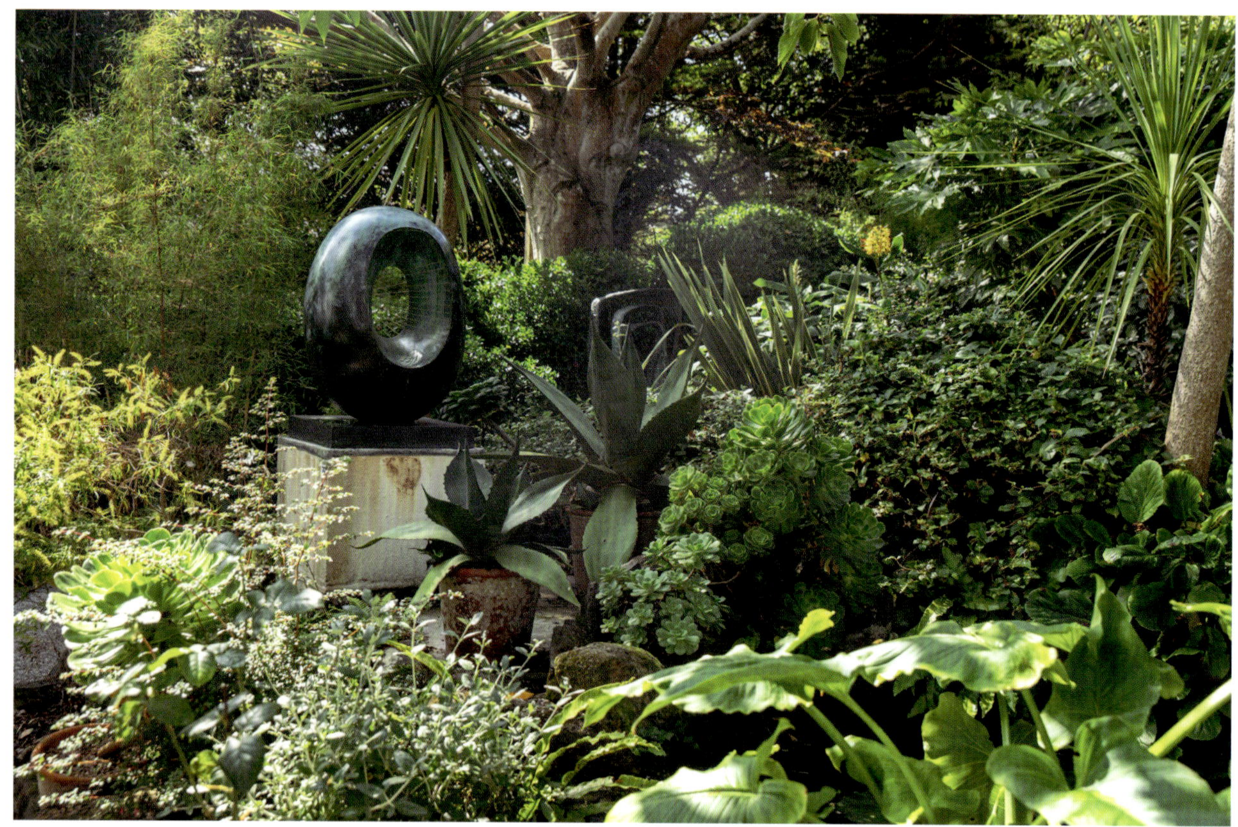

Spring 1966

Figure for Landscape 1959–60 (right)
The title of this work suggests that Hepworth may have imagined it sited in the countryside. She often referred to the importance of the figure in the landscape and to the relationship between the individual human body and the wide environment. In her work she sought to say something affirmative about this relationship, about being in the world. In reducing the figure to a simple, shrouded form she obscures any definite identity, allowing it to stand for everyone.

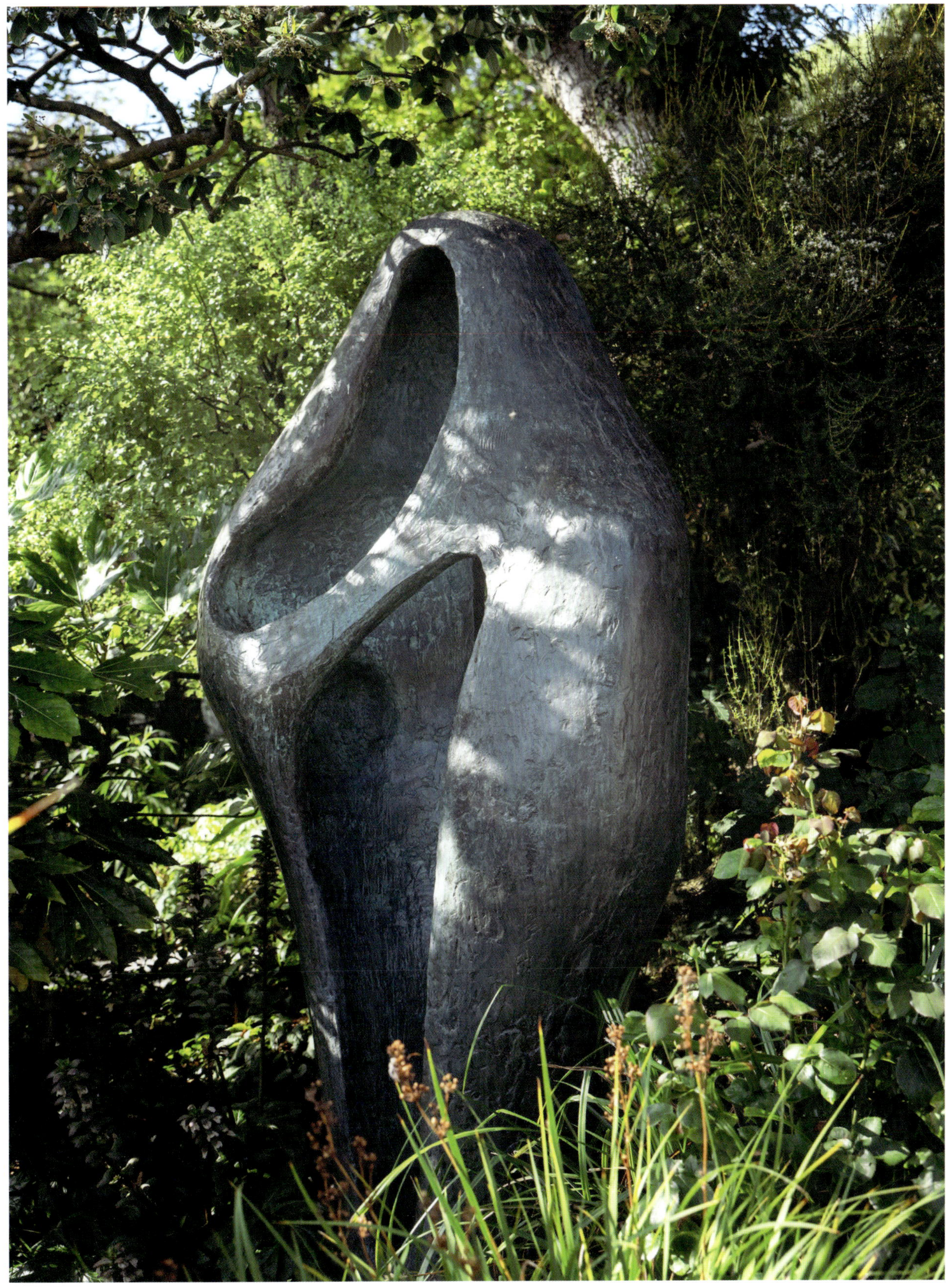

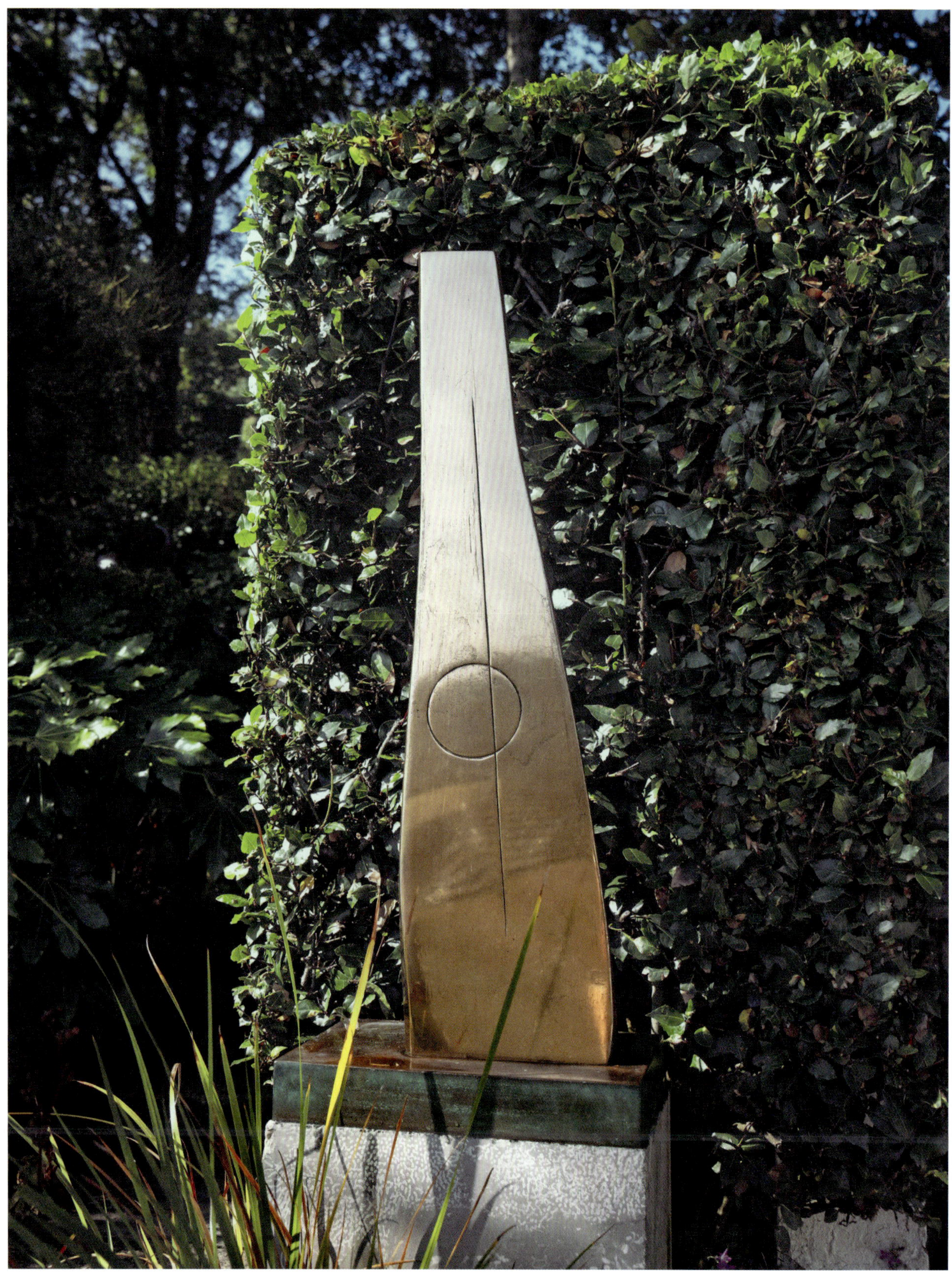

Shaft and Circle 1973

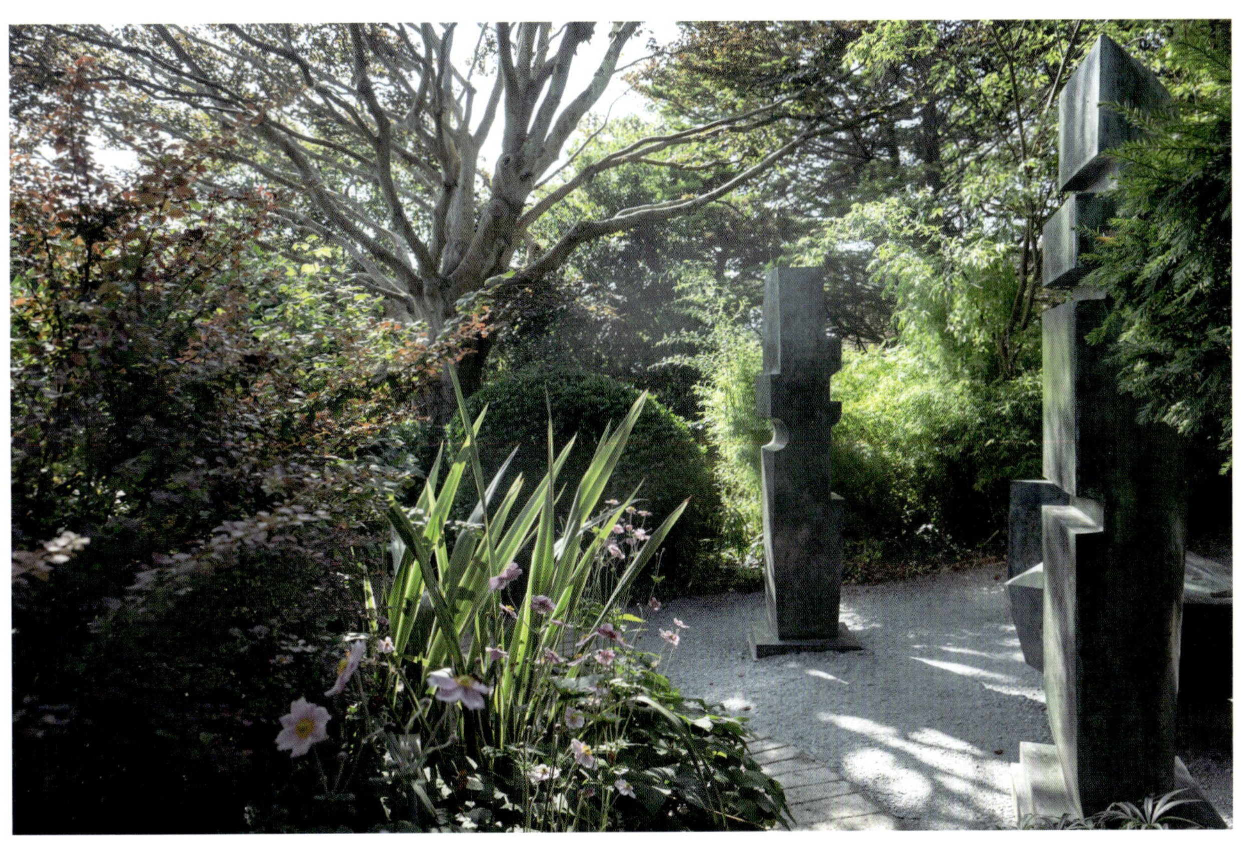

Autumn

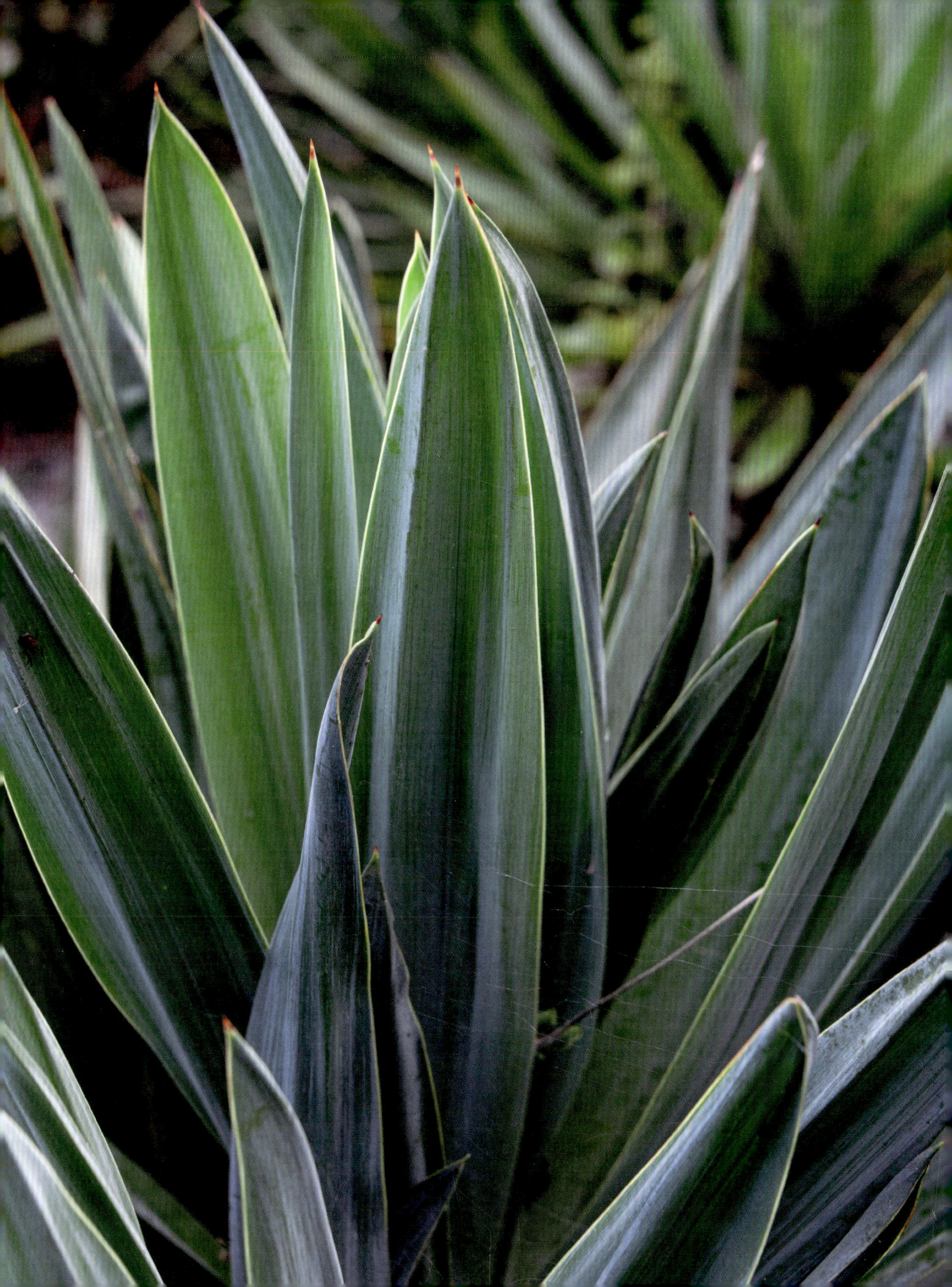

River Form 1965, cast 1973 (right)
Some of Hepworth's bronzes, such as this one, were derived from wood carvings. The interiors of these were often painted and the contrast of outer and inner surfaces was echoed in her patination of the bronze. It was, perhaps, the horizontality of the sculpture and the eddy-like spiralling of its holes that suggested the title. In the garden at Trewyn, the collecting of rainwater within the sculpture adds an extra dimension which is especially appropriate to the title.

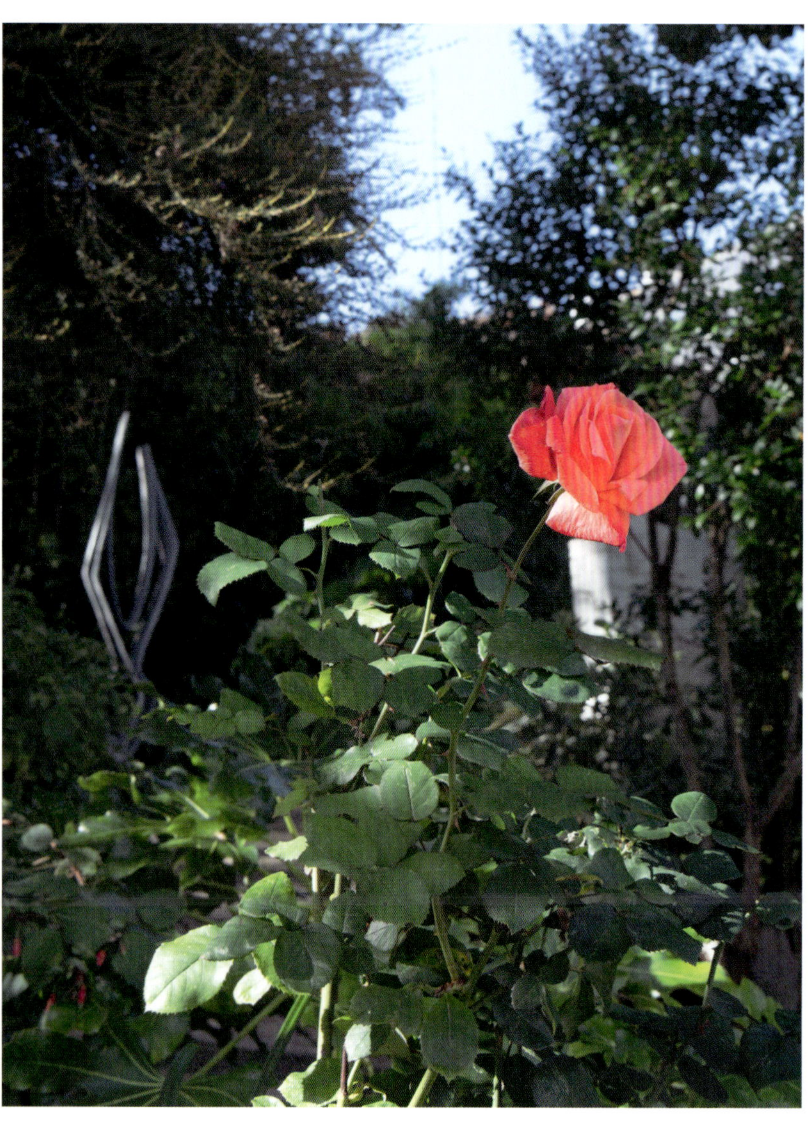

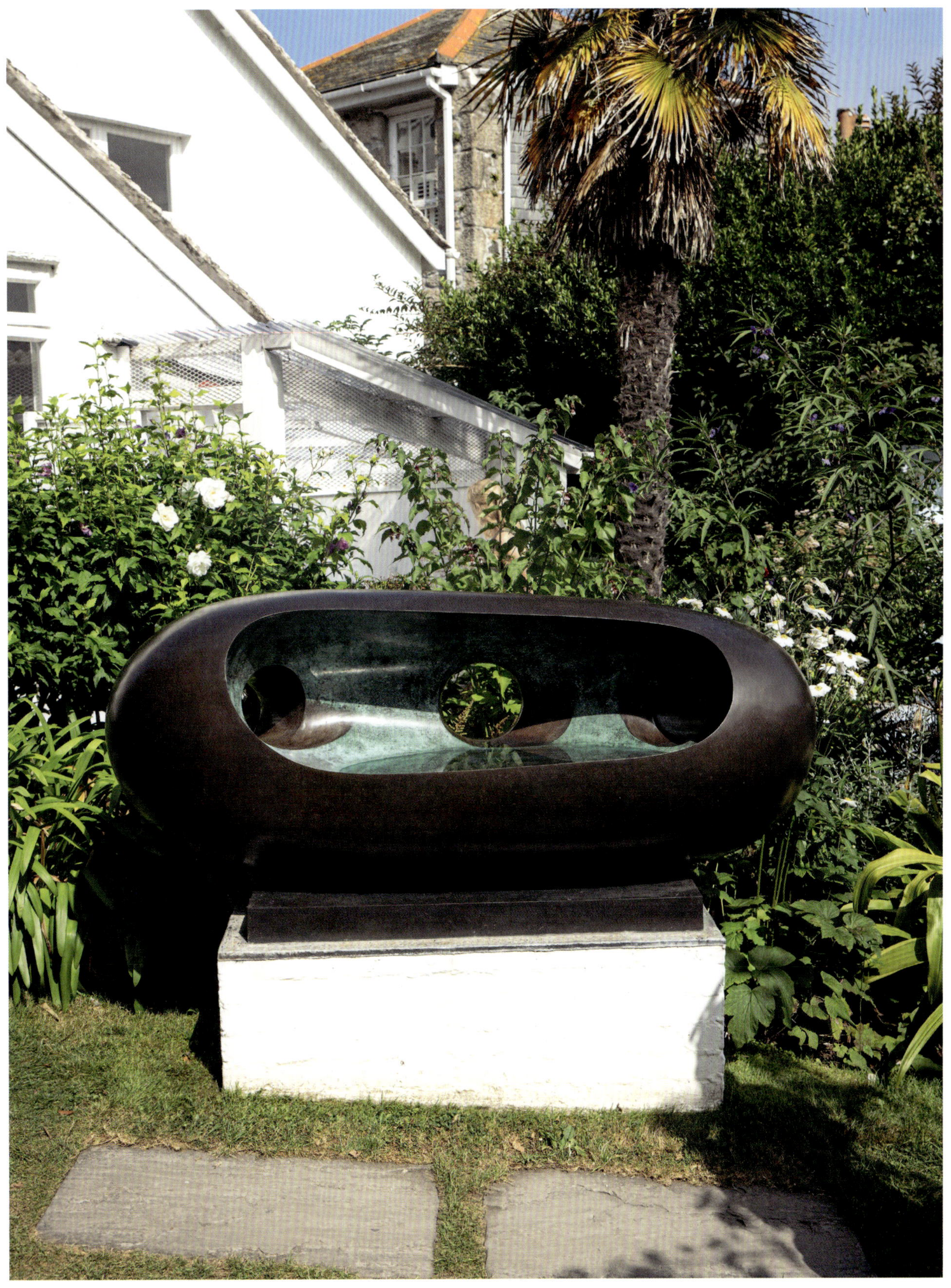

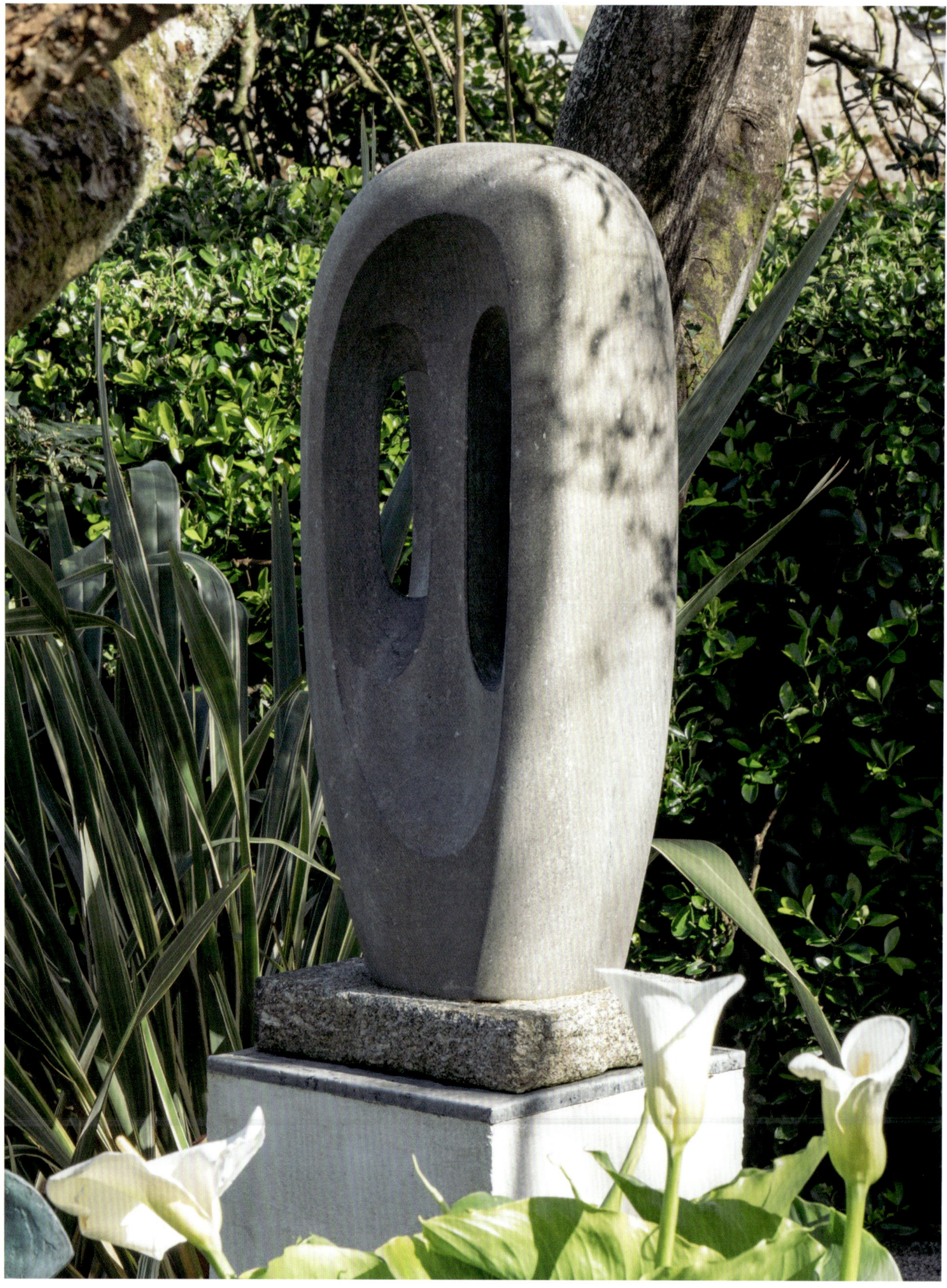

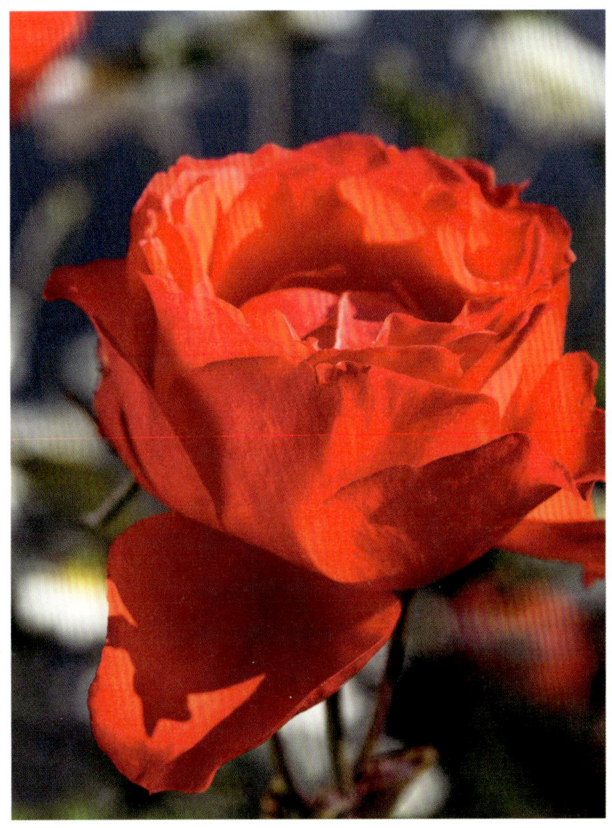

19 Roses

Stone Sculpture (Fugue II) 1956 (left)
For Hepworth, the form of a sculpture was dictated by the material from which it was carved, and she wrote of the sculptor's search for the work's 'structure of rhythm'. Comparisons of sculpture with music were common for her, as the title of this work indicates. The limestone of *Stone Sculpture* is characterised by numerous fossils. Originally, the stone was more highly finished, but long display outside has weathered its surface.

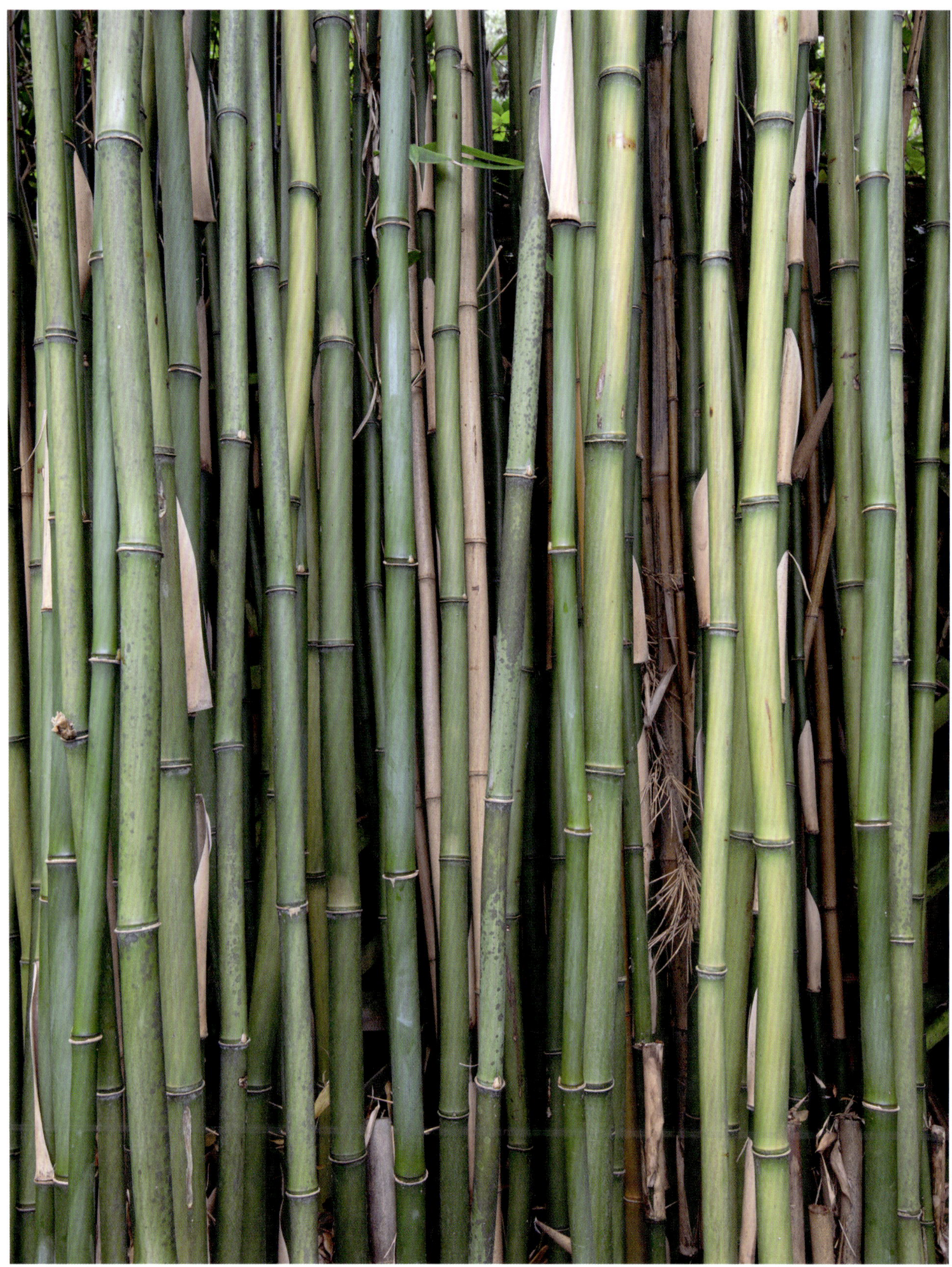

20 *Phyllostachys nigra* f. 'Henonis' bamboo

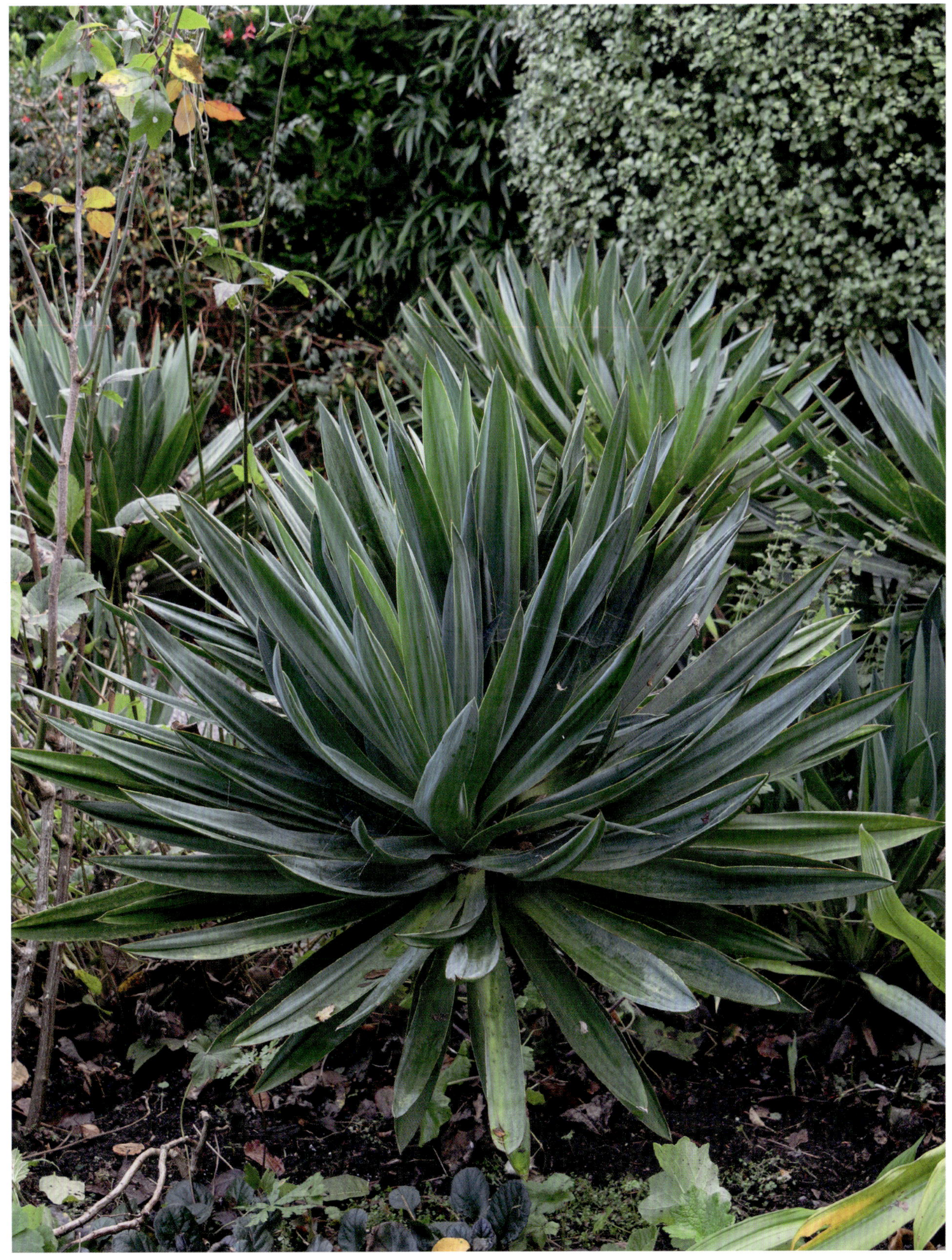

21 *Yucca gloriosa* yucca, see also p.61

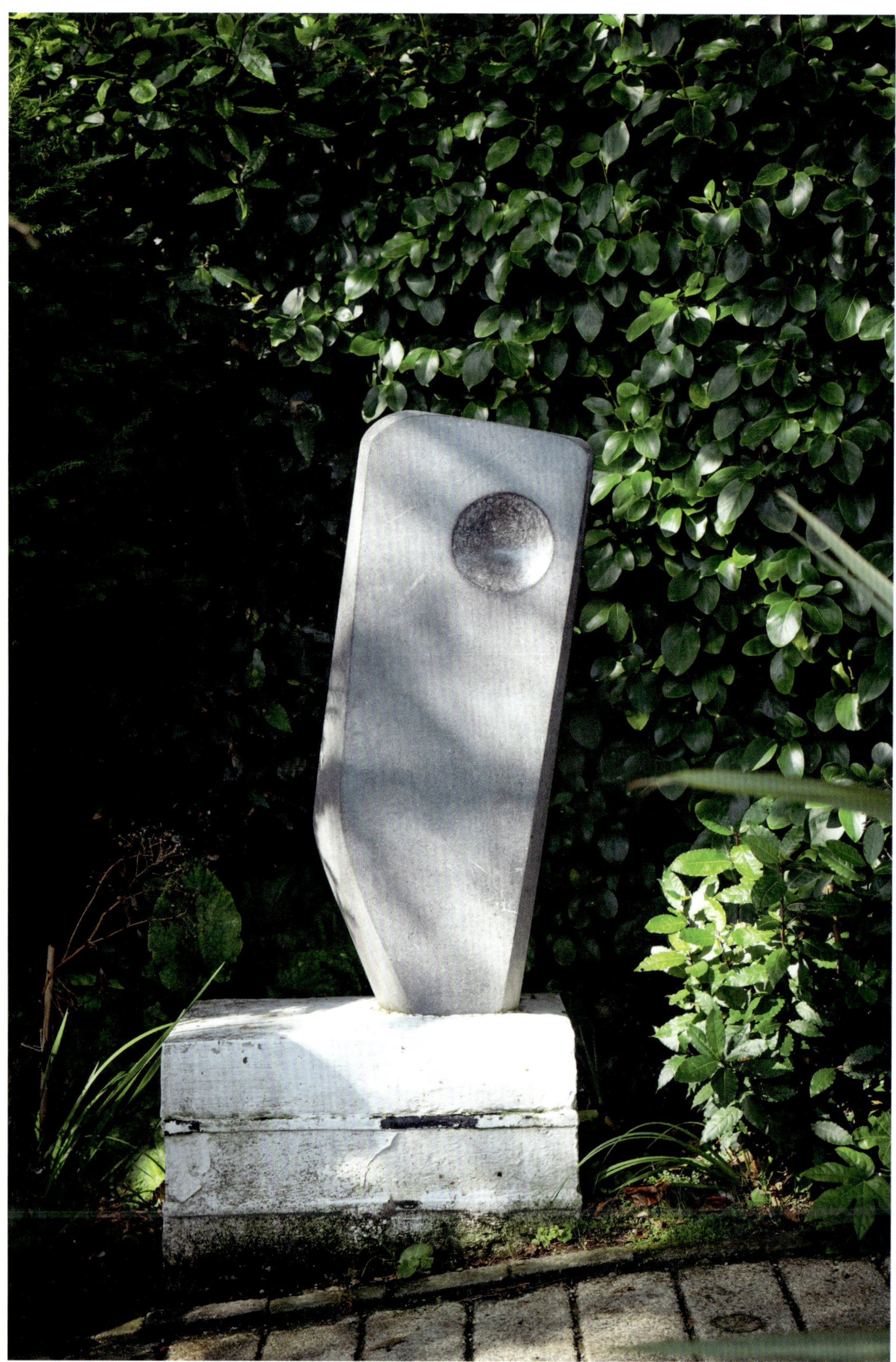

Poised Form 1951–2, reworked 1957

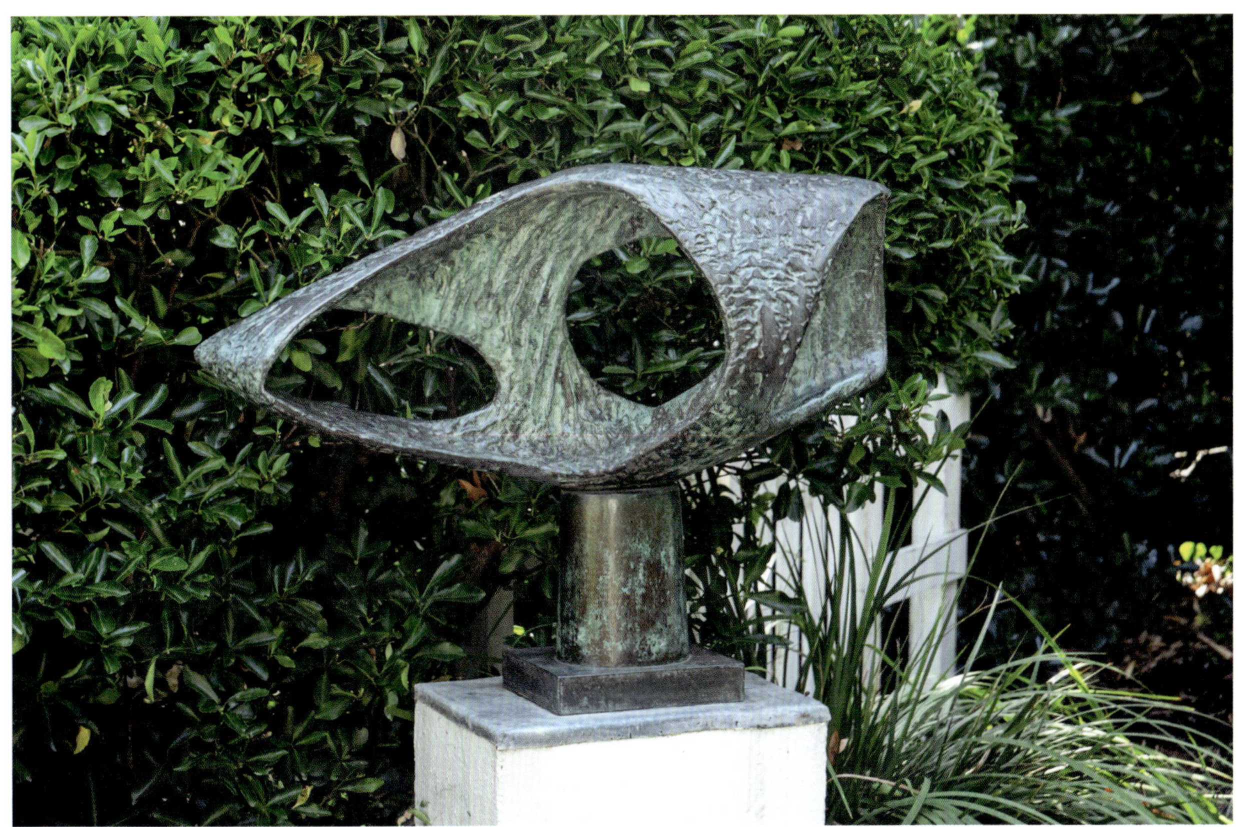

Bronze Form (Patmos) 1962–3

19 Roses
According to her family and friends, roses were Barbara Hepworth's favourite flowers. When she acquired Trewyn in 1949 there were three geometrically shaped rose beds that dominated the lower garden. She did away with the formal beds, kept most of the roses, and introduced meandering borders and other plants, to create a more naturalistic garden. Today roses remain a favourite at Trewyn, and include floribundas, some red, white and one orange hybrid tea. The variety of roses in the museum garden makes it difficult to specify all their individual requirements, but a few basic guidelines can be followed. Most roses are hardy, prefer open, sunny positions, and need shelter from salt-laden or strong winds. The soil should be moist, fertile and well drained, and the rose should be fed in winter or early spring to ensure high-quality blooms. Pruning varies according to type and sometimes to the gardener's preference.

20 *Phyllostachys nigra f.* 'Henonis' bamboo
Bamboo can be clump-forming or running, the latter being invasive. *Phyllostachys nigra* f. Henonis is a running bamboo, but fortunately is relatively well behaved in the museum garden. There are several bamboos throughout that can rustle in the wind, providing a fluidity of encapsulating sound. The largest specimen provides a beautiful foil to *Conversation with Magic Stones* 1973 with its majestic canes, the leaves on which can be removed up to a certain height to enhance this quality. The only other pruning required is the cutting down of tired-looking old stems, which should be cut right down to ground level, but can then be used as supports for other plants. East Asian in origin, bamboo is a popular plant of which there are many varieties available–most of these like rich, light, moist soils. Nearly all bamboos die after flowering which fortunately only happens after perhaps sixty or a hundred years. Thus, if a bamboo does flower, it is important to save the seed. They need a sheltered position as they can be badly damaged by wind. Bamboos come in many different sizes and colour stems – it is possible to find one suitable for most gardens.

21 *Yucca gloriosa* yucca
Yuccas come from the southern United States, Mexico and the Caribbean, and were originally thought to be a member of the cassava family–yucca is the Caribbean word for cassava. They have many common names including Adam's needle and Spanish bayonet, and were introduced by Augustus Smith to his sub-tropical gardens on Tresco in 1857, probably from Kew Gardens in London. Yuccas look exotic but are fully hardy. Stiff, blue-grey, sword-shaped leaves are carried in a rosette above a short, stout stem. The leaf tips are formidably sharp, and the rosette of leaves can reach a height of sixty to ninety centimetres. During the summer a tall flower stalk develops from the centre of the rosette, which will bear up to forty pendent tulip-shaped flowers in the autumn. These are creamy white, flushed with a dusky red on the outside. The flower spike should be cut back when spent, leaving only about five centimetres above the leaves. Yuccas take about three years to become established, can be grown in large containers or open ground, like any well-drained soil, and enjoy full sun or light shade. Among the most valuable of architectural plants in the museum garden, they provide an energising juxtaposition with the more rounded shapes of the sculptures.

22 *Pelargoniums*
Bred from several South African species, pelargoniums are frost-tender and will not tolerate temperatures below zero degrees Celsius. Usually grown in pots in the home, conservatory or greenhouse, they are, however, extremely easy to propagate from cuttings, so it is simple to grow new plants. They come in a huge range of sizes and in every shade of pink, from clear white to dark, velvety burgundy. Most have a long flowering season, and quickly sprout new growth if pruned. At the museum garden there are a number of regal pelargoniums and a classic single red, perhaps 'Ville de Paris'. The two varieties shown here are *Pelargonium zonale* 'Fireworks' on the left and *Pelargonium* x *domesticum* 'Ann Hoysted' on the right. *Pelargonium* x *domesticum*, or regal pelargoniums, have been around for centuries and are perhaps least suited to outdoor use, but make excellent house or conservatory specimens.

23 *Mahonia japonica* Japanese mahonia
Collected by the 'plant hunter' Robert Fortune in China in the 1840s, *Mahonia japonica* is an evergreen shrub with rosettes of deep-green shiny and spiky leaves, and forms a rather dense shape. It eventually reaches a height of about two metres and a similar spread. It filters wind effectively, but its true value becomes apparent just before Christmas when the rosettes of flower spikes, often fifteen centimetres long, begin to open. Delicate lemon-yellow flowers, that are a magnet for bees, brighten the mahonia from December to late February; their scent carries well and always intrigues visitors to Trewyn. The berries that follow are a deep purple-blue and are much loved by birds, and if you're fortunate, by the occasional brambling overwintering in Cornwall. Mahonias are fully hardy, preferring shade or semi-shade.

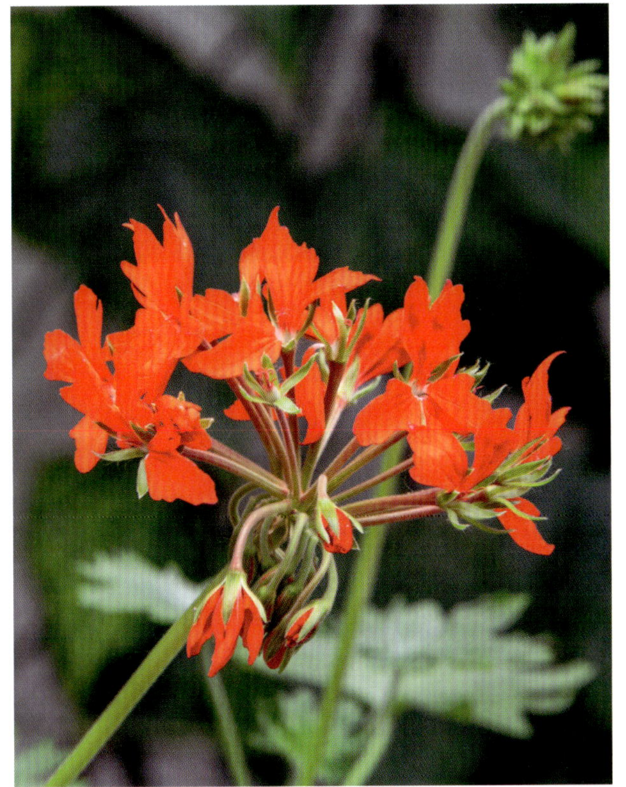 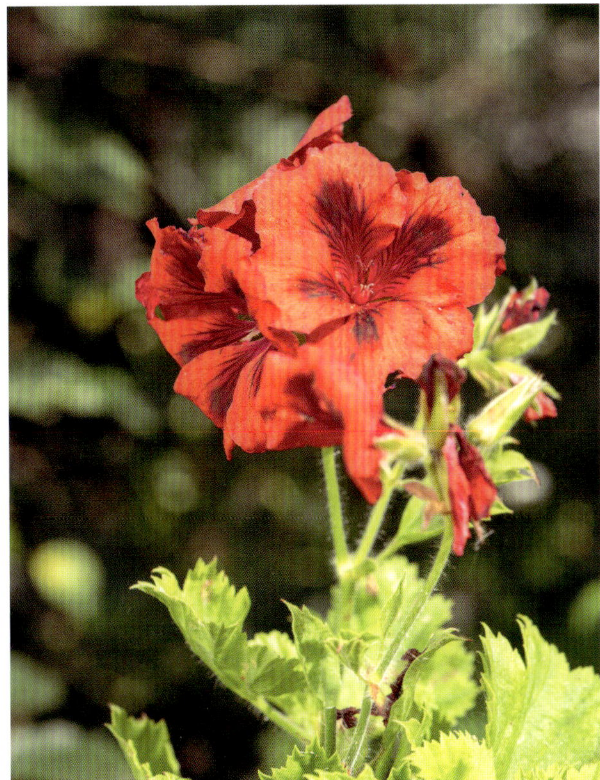

22   *Pelargoniums*

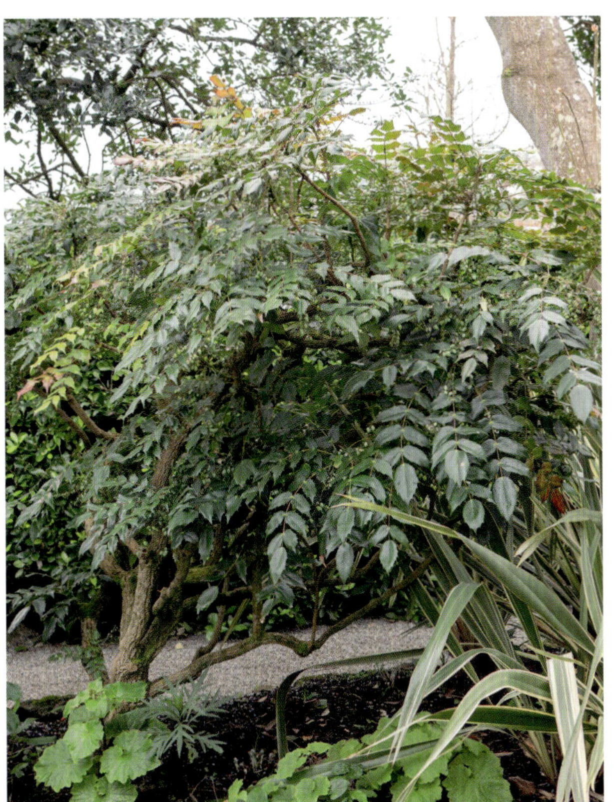 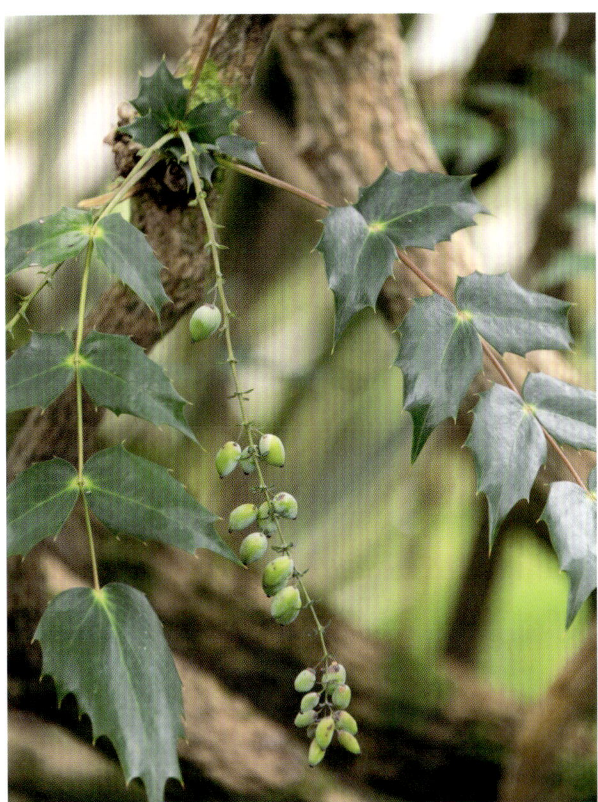

23   *Mahonia japonica* Japanese mahonia

Sphere with Inner form 1963 (right)
Sculptures in which one small form is enclosed within another larger one had
been common in Hepworth's work since the 1930s. She drew attention to the
relationship between inside and outside: 'a nut in its shell or of a child in the womb,
or in the structure of shells or of crystals'. These works, then, evoke a sense
of growth, nurture and protection. While this reflects Hepworth's common use
of natural forms and processes, such concerns have been specifically related
to her particular view as a woman and a mother.

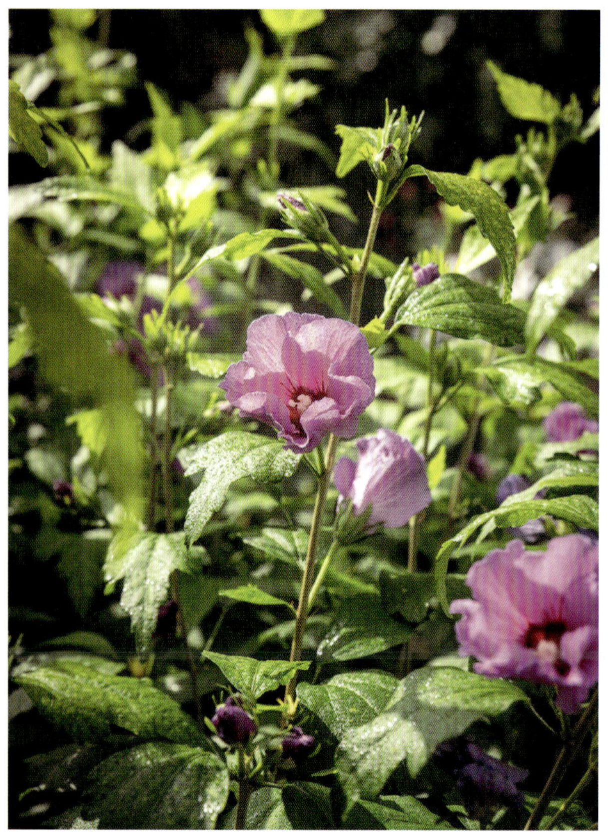

24   *Hibiscus syriacus* 'Woodbridge' hardy hibiscus

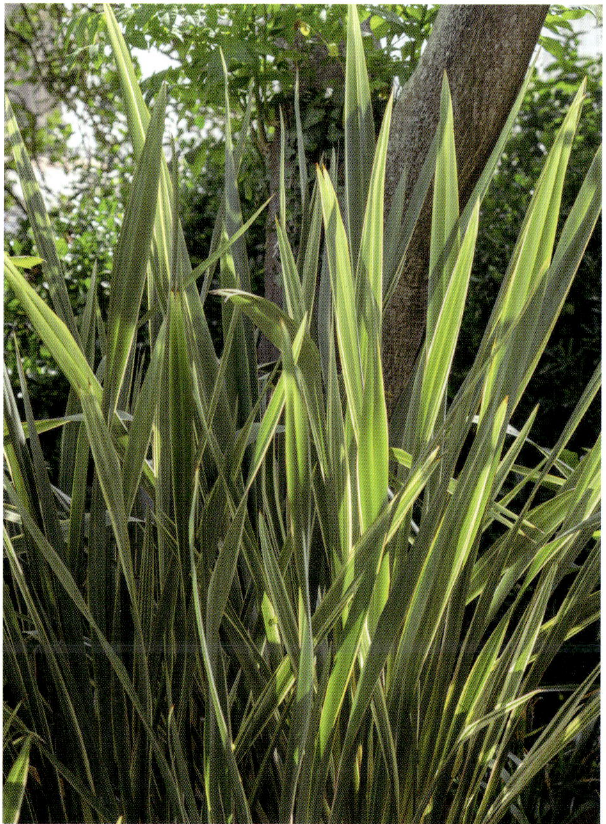

25   *Phormium tenax* 'Variegatum' New Zealand flax

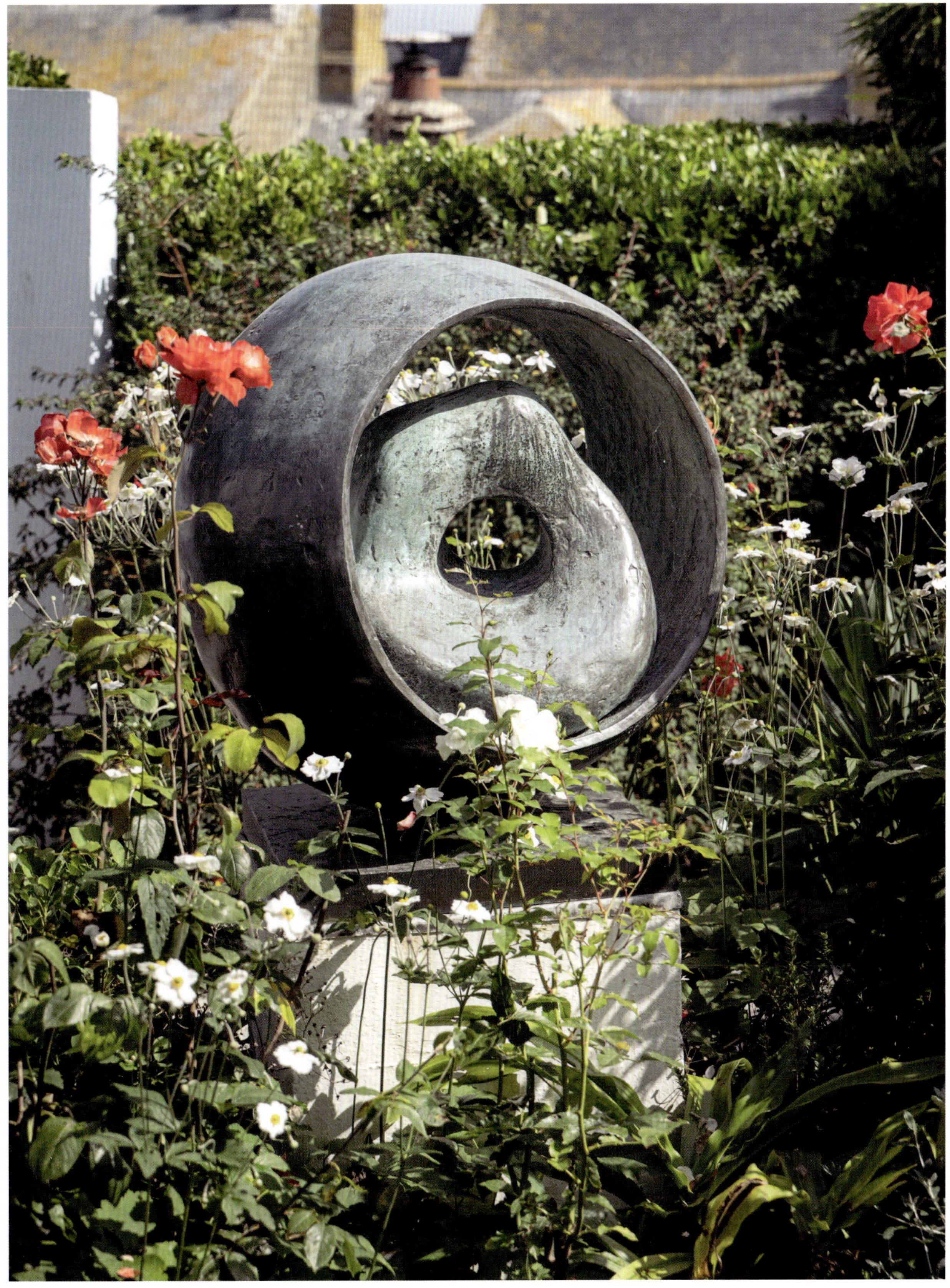

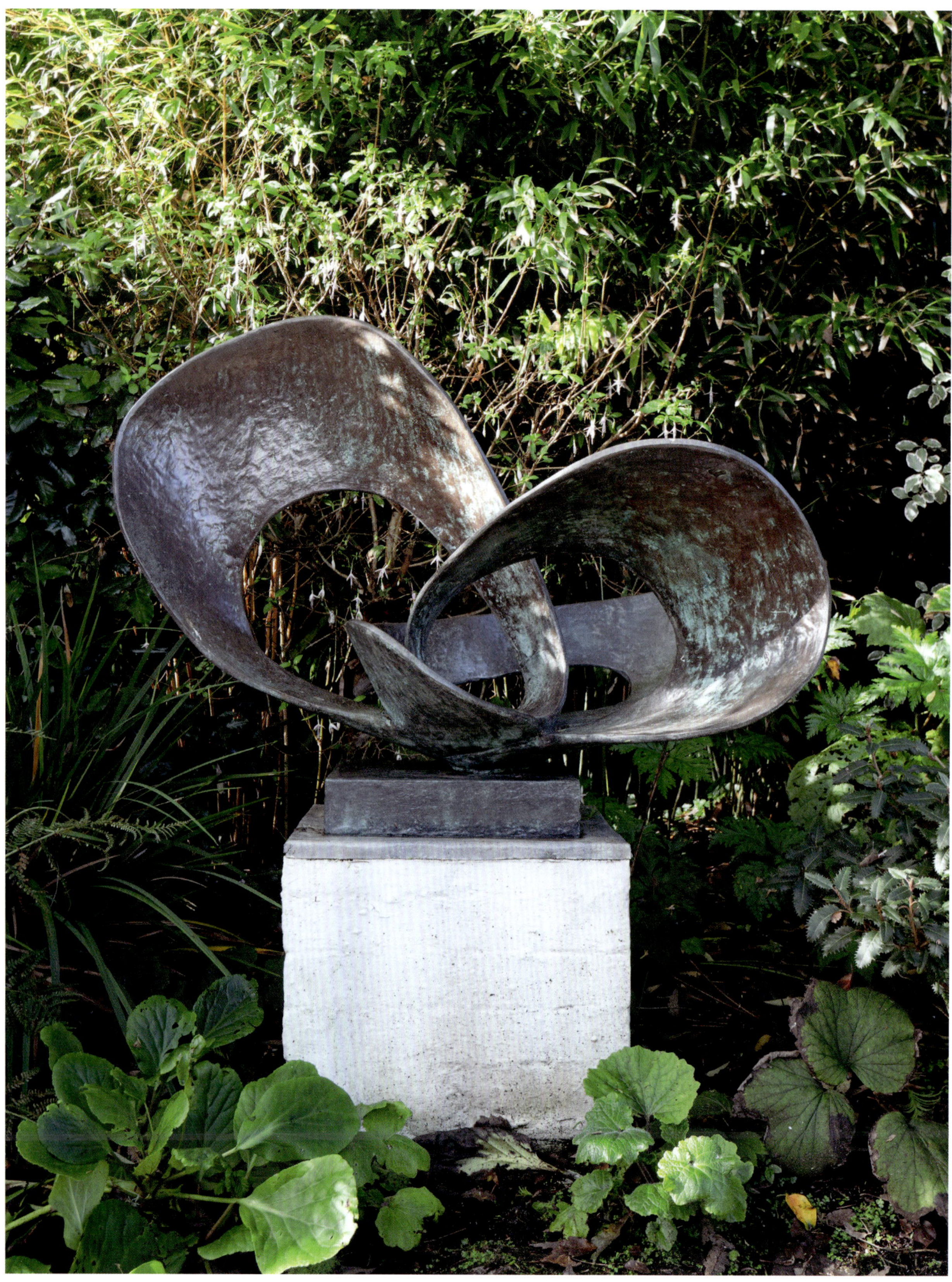

Forms in Movement (Pavan) 1956–9, cast 1967

24   *Hibiscus syriacus* 'Woodbridge' hardy hibiscus
Native to China and Japan, *Hibiscus syriacus* was first
collected in Syria, hence its name. A deciduous shrub,
it reaches three metres in height and eventually, a similar
spread. It is late to leaf–often well into May–but the
stems remain attractive until then. The deeply lobed
leaves are a fresh lime-green when they first appear,
maturing to a dark green. Abundant flowers open from
July to October, each lasting only a day or two.
'Woodbridge', one of the most beautiful of the outdoor
varieties, has open, trumpet-shaped flowers seven to
ten centimetres across. The petals have a glossy
sheen, and the blooms are a vibrant purple-pink with a
dark magenta eye. Though much hardier than it looks,
the hibiscus will not tolerate cold winds or a late frost.
Generally, it needs full sun, a well drained soil, and
requires little pruning–if desired, it can be thinned and
reduced in the late spring.

25   *Phormium tenax* 'Variegatum' New Zealand flax
An evergreen and robust perennial that is native to New
Zealand, the Maori people traditionally used the fibres
for making items such as baskets and rope, as it is one
of the strongest natural fibres known. It makes a
dramatic statement in the museum garden with bold,
erect, sword-like foliage up to two metres high that
makes a striking contrast with the other planting and
sculptures. In summer it is topped by a flowering stalk
with panicles of tubular red flowers that are a good
source of pollen and nectar for bees and other
pollinating insects–these are followed by sturdy seed
heads. A great coastal plant, providing year-round
architectural structure that needs relatively little pruning,
except for removing discoloured or dead leaves, and it
is important to watch out for mealybug around the base.

Winter

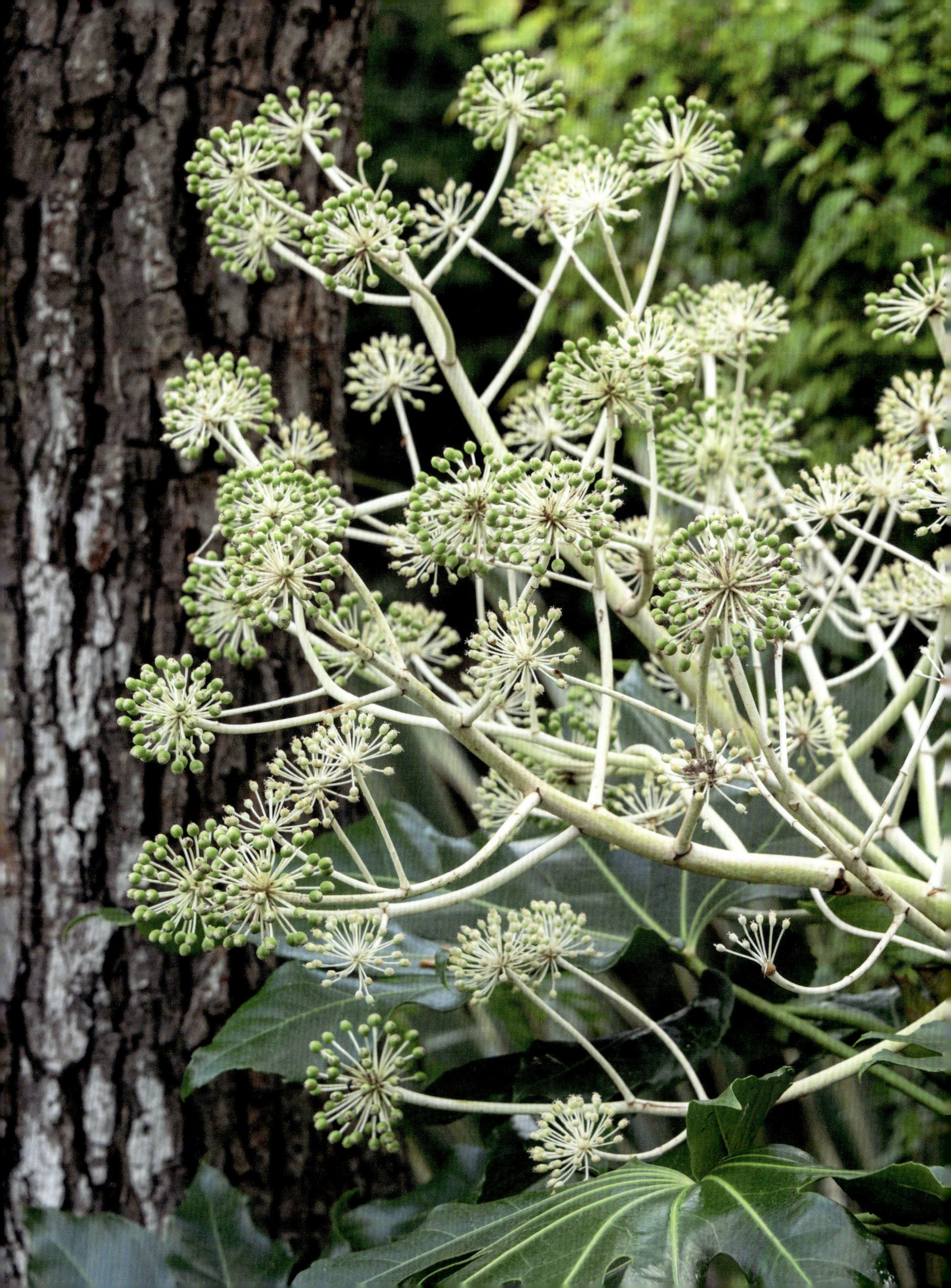

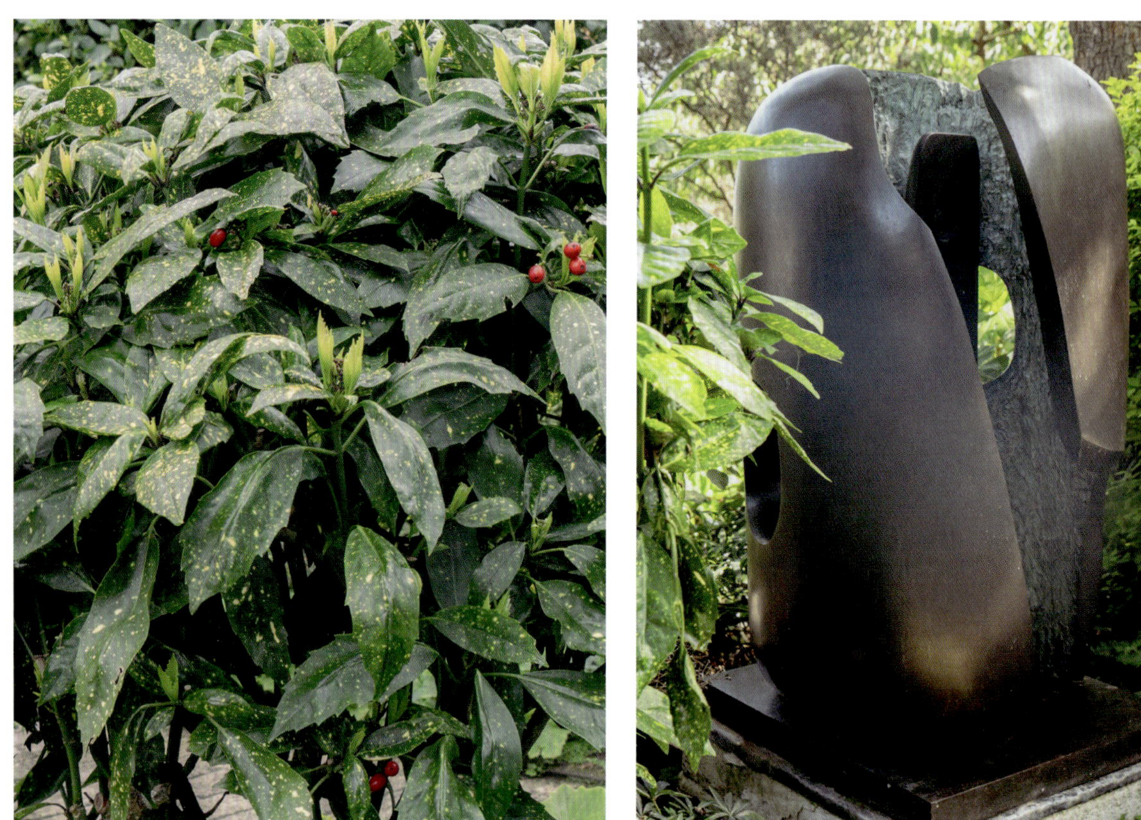

26   *Aucuba japonica* 'Variegata' variegated Japanese laurel and *Hollow Form with Inner Form* 1968

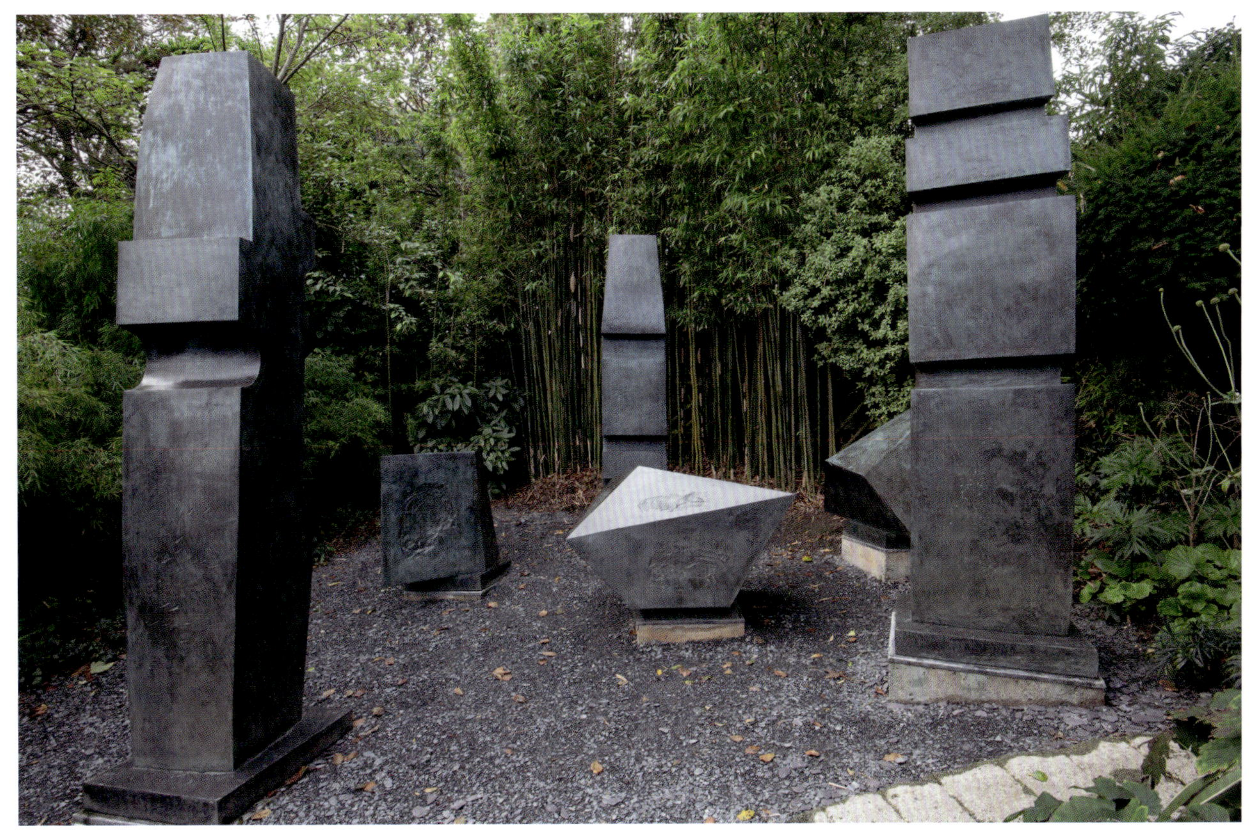

Conversation with Magic Stones 1973 (above)
This was Hepworth's last major bronze. Despite ill health, she was able to oversee the position of each piece. Though apparently abstract, the vertical elements suggest figures. Their inter-relationship stands as a metaphor for human interaction, while a tension is established between them and the smaller stones, which may be seen as embodiments of metaphysical or magical forces. The group has also been compared with the circles of standing stones that can be seen in the landscape close to St Ives.

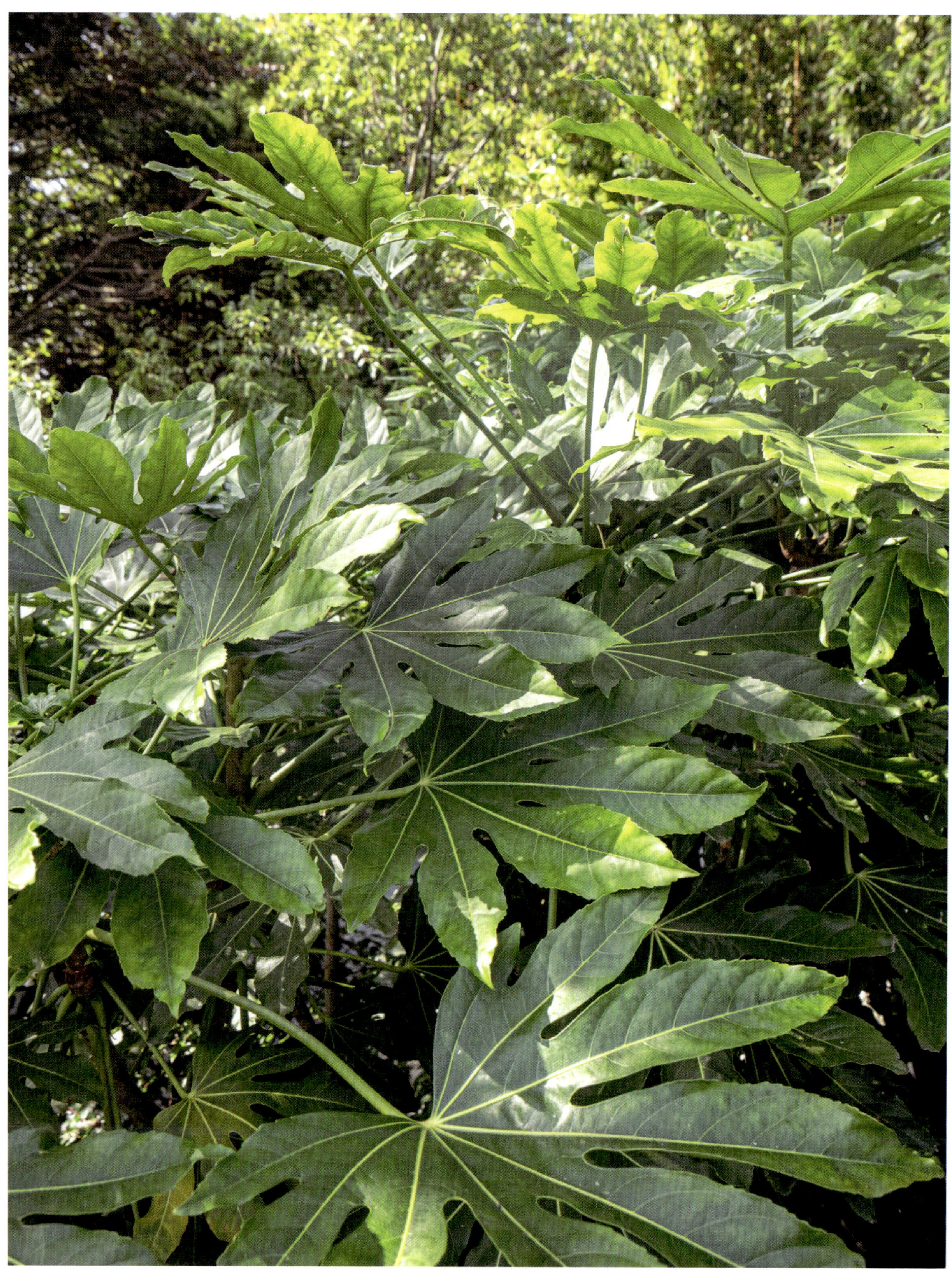

27   *Fatsia japonica* Japanese aralia, see also p.77.

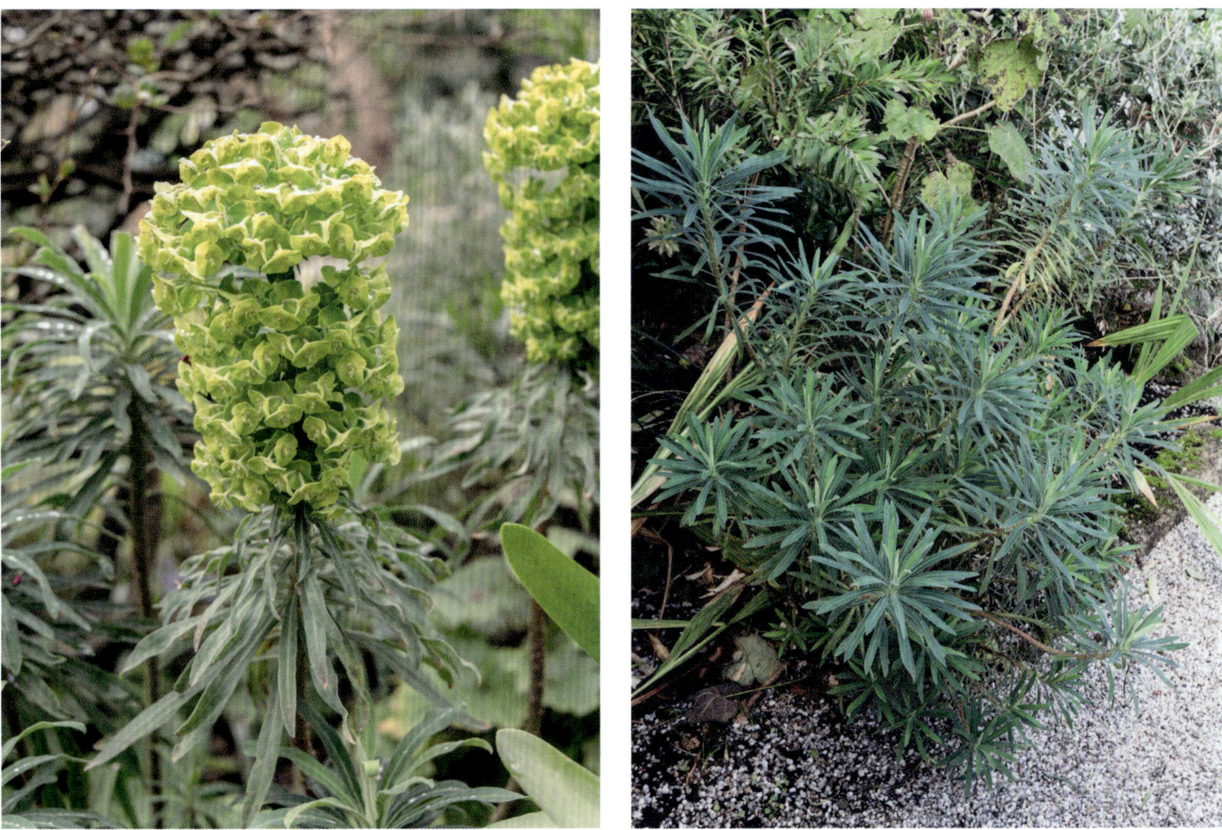

28 *Euphorbia characias* subsp. *wulfenii* euphorbia, shown in spring on the left, and in winter on the right.

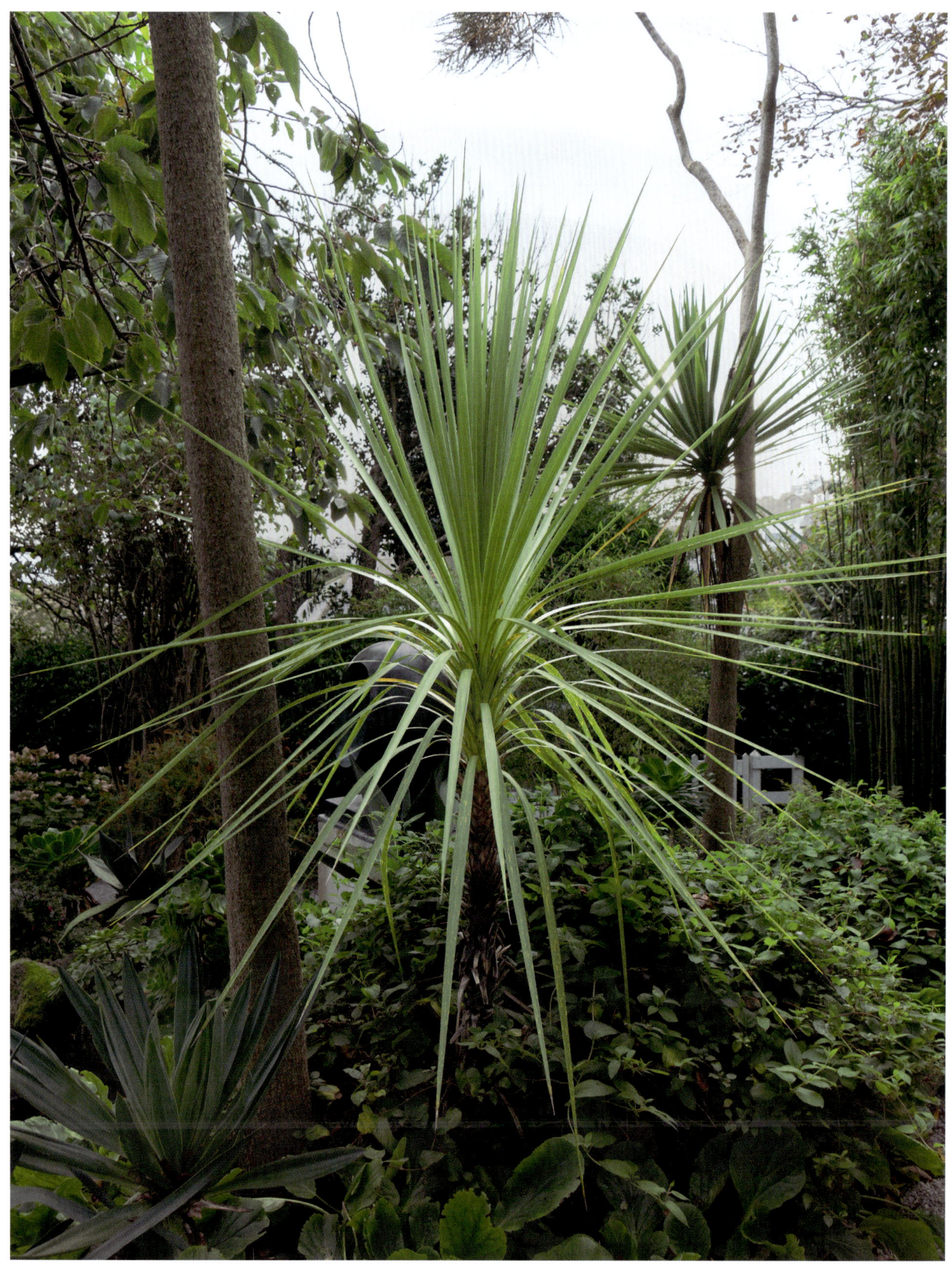

29 *Cordyline australis* Australian cabbage palm

26 *Aucuba japonica* 'Variegata'
     variegated Japanese laurel
A handsome evergreen shrub with large, pointed oval
leaves, *Aucuba* thrives almost anywhere, even in deep
shade under trees or in city areas. In the museum garden,
along with numerous other trees and shrubs, sensitive
pruning and thinning is undertaken, to retain sight lines
and balance, and consequently the light levels and
atmosphere that Barbara Hepworth so carefully curated.
'Variegata' is one of the most valuable forms; its glossy,
rich green leaves are heavily speckled with a sharp
yellow. The flowers, blooming through March and April,
are small and insignificant, but a female variety is
capable of bearing attractive oval red berries in small
clusters from autumn through winter if a male laurel is
within pollinating distance. To cover a large, shady patch
of garden and ensure the maximum show of berries,
plant three females to each male. Spotted laurel forms
a rounded bush from two to three metres in height and
spread, and should succeed in any garden soil.

27 *Fatsia japonica* Japanese aralia
Also known as the false castor oil plant, this evergreen
shrub looks remarkably exotic in an English garden.
It carries globe-shaped clusters of small, creamy white
flowers from October to December, that are an
important source of pollen and nectar for bees into the
winter months. These are followed by dull green berries
that turn matt black as winter progresses, which are an
important and nutritious winter food resource for birds.
The dark, glossy green leaves are deeply lobed and
often more than thirty centimetres across; they will look
their best when grown in partial to full shade. *Fatsia
japonica* needs shelter from strong winds, especially in
colder areas, but thrives in the south and west of
England, and is completely frost hardy. Pruning is only
necessary to retain balance with surrounding planting,
and should be carried out in spring.

28 *Euphorbia characias* subsp. *wulfenii* euphorbia
Euphorbias are a huge genus, with over 2000 species
worldwide. In the UK they have a range of evocative
folk-names such as wolf's bane and purging spurge
(a name indicating the genus' historical uses as both
a purgative and a poison – waterproof gloves and eye
protection are recommended when cutting or handling
euphorbias). *E. characias* is native to Greece and the
Balkans, but has been cultivated in British gardens
since the early nineteenth century. It is fully hardy and
forms a clump of tough, upright stems ninety
centimetres high or more, clothed in long, narrow,
blue-green leaves, giving an effect rather like a fat,
green, bottle brush. Euphorbias flower from December
until mid-June, but the flowers are insignificant. Like the
poinsettia, they are valued for their flower bracts, which
are a bright yellowish-green, cup-shaped, and form at
the top of the stem. *E. characias* will flower annually,

producing bract and flower heads up to fifteen
centimetres tall at the tip of the stems. Each bract is
further enhanced by a dark burgundy centre within the
cup. Old stems that have finished flowering should be
cut back to ground level after going to seed, if new
plants are desired the following season.

29 *Cordyline australis* Australian cabbage palm
One of the first plants introduced to the UK by
Augustus Smith (1804–72), cordylines, also known as
draceana, are a familiar feature of many of Britain's
seaside resorts, making wonderfully impressive trees
that evoke memories of idyllic summer holidays. A
Cordyline australis in a favourable position in open
ground will reach about five metres or more, with the
'topknot' of leaves spreading to about one and a half
metres. The oldest of the sword-shaped leaves
discolour and are shed in late autumn to free the
plant's resources for the next season's growth. Stiff,
branched panicles up to ninety centimetres long, carry
the small, heavily scented, creamy flowers in mid-
summer; these are followed by a mass of spherical
fruits. Cordylines often benefit greatly from regular
foliar feeding with Epsom salts.
   Sadly, the cordylines in the museum garden have
been in decline for several years now, mainly due to the
taller trees out-competing them. If plants are lost due to
disease, climate change, or changing conditions within
the garden, then it becomes most important to maintain
a 'sense of place'; that is the atmosphere and feeling
that the garden creates for visitors, staff, family
members and other stakeholders. It is maintaining this
sense of place, and historical authenticity, that
underpins all Hepworth Museum Garden management.
This concept is illustrated in this instance, where the
cordylines are in decline due to changing conditions,
and as such are being replaced by *Trachycarpus
fortunei*, the other more shade tolerant palm of the
garden (see p.89). In the process, they are providing a
similar tropical look to the lost cordylines.

Coré 1955–6, cast 1960 (right)
The white marble carving from which this piece was cast once stood in a similar position in the garden. That original material is, perhaps, better suited to the work's title, which is a type of ancient Greek female figure sculpture. Its organic curves, however, are very different to the rigid verticality of such antique objects. Though the arc and circle near the top may suggest a face, they may also refer to the sun and moon, standing as fundamental forces of nature.

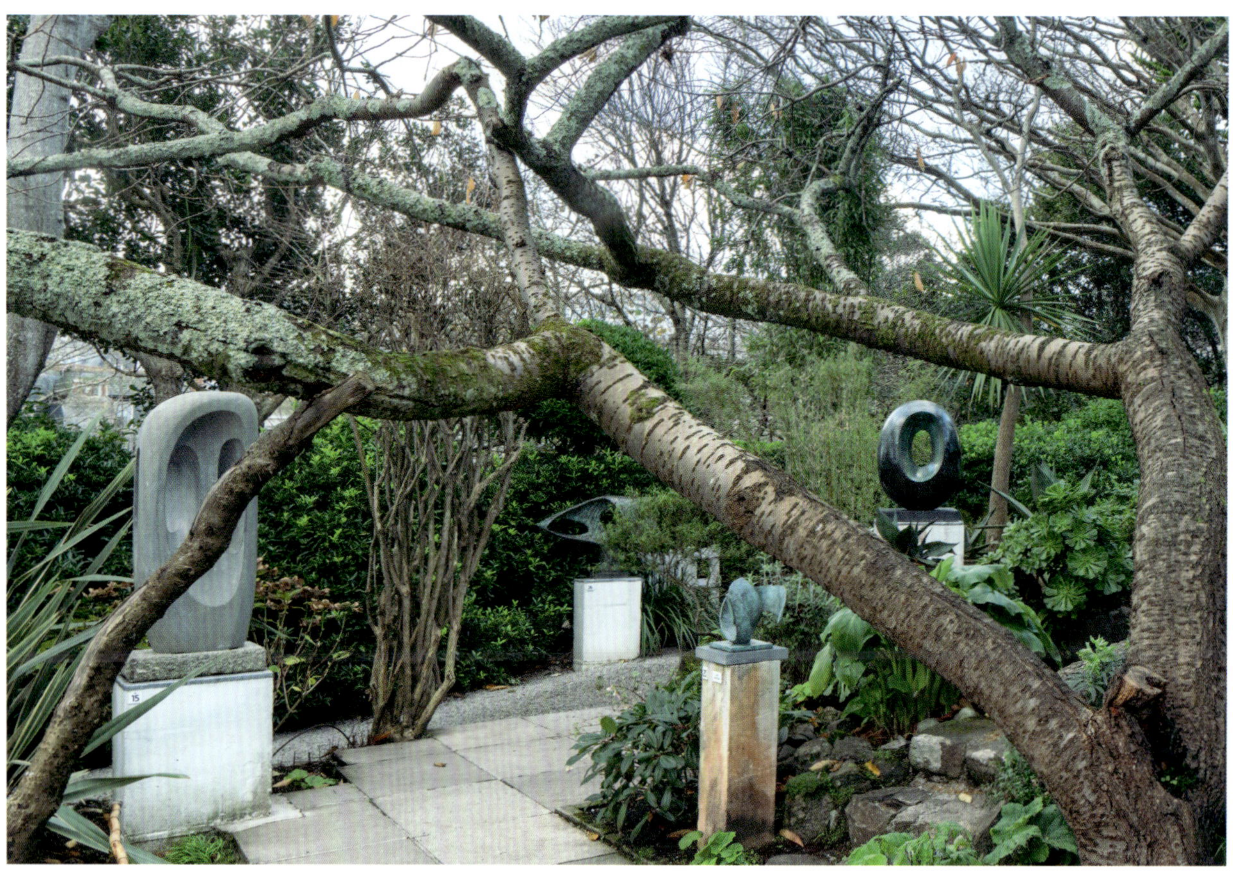

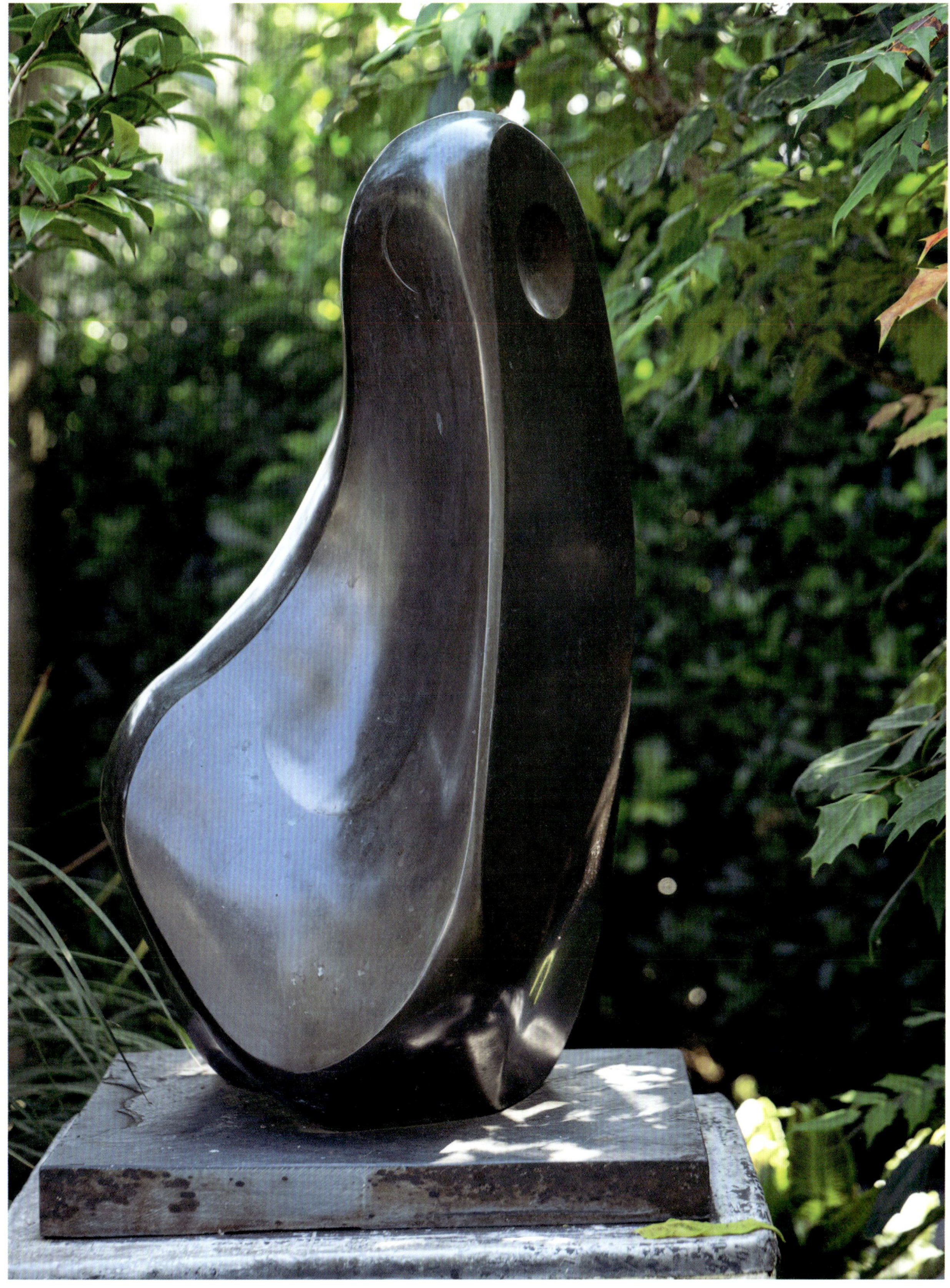

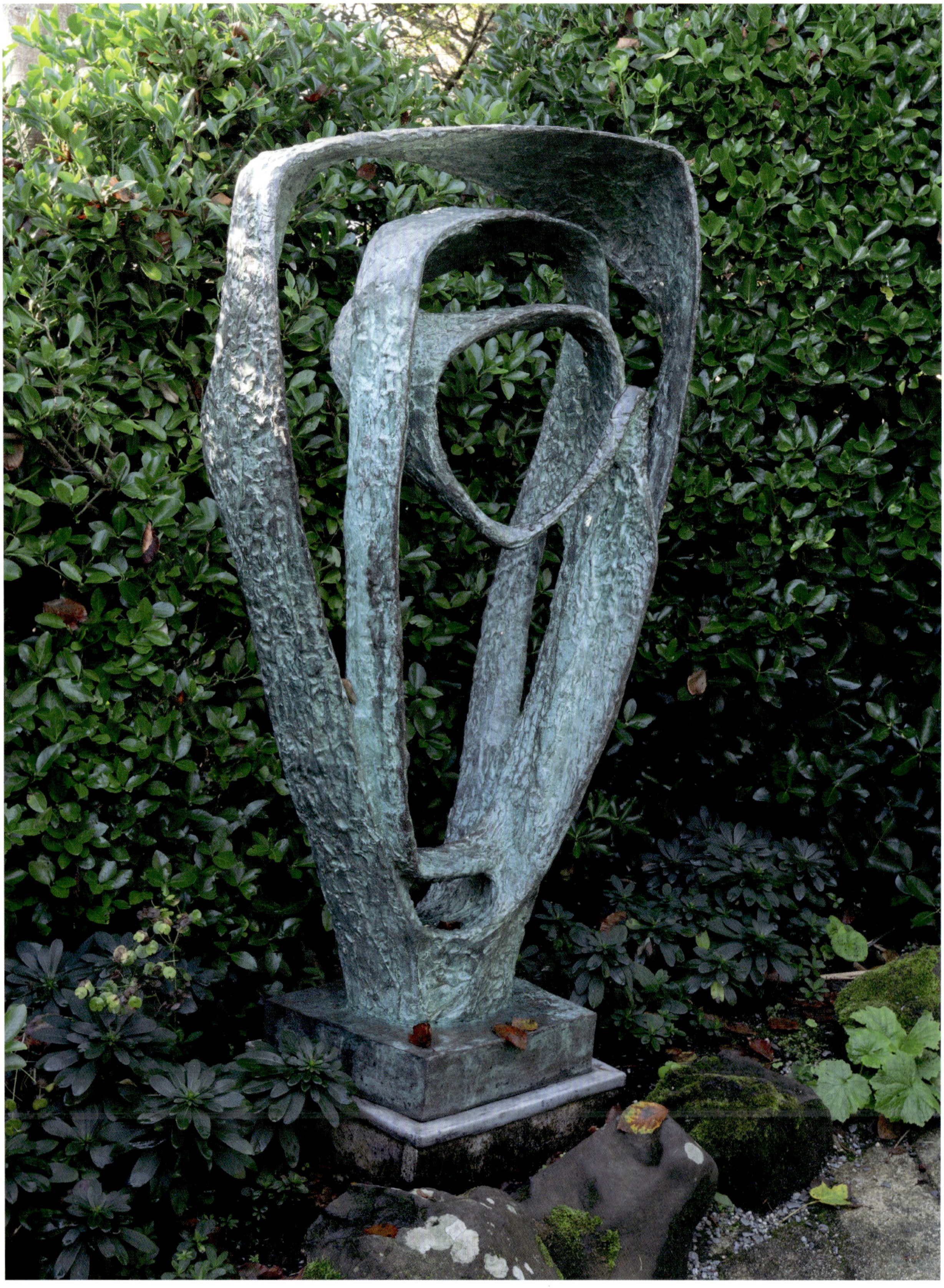

Garden Sculpture (Model for Meridian) 1958 (left)
An intermediate stage in the development of the two and a half metre high *Meridian* for a new building in London, the form of this sculpture evokes ideas of organic growth with which Hepworth hoped to relieve the stark geometry of the architecture. The sculpture was made in several sizes, the initial idea being fashioned from pipe-cleaners. Both the expanding forms and the highly textured surface suggest the natural associations made explicit by its title.

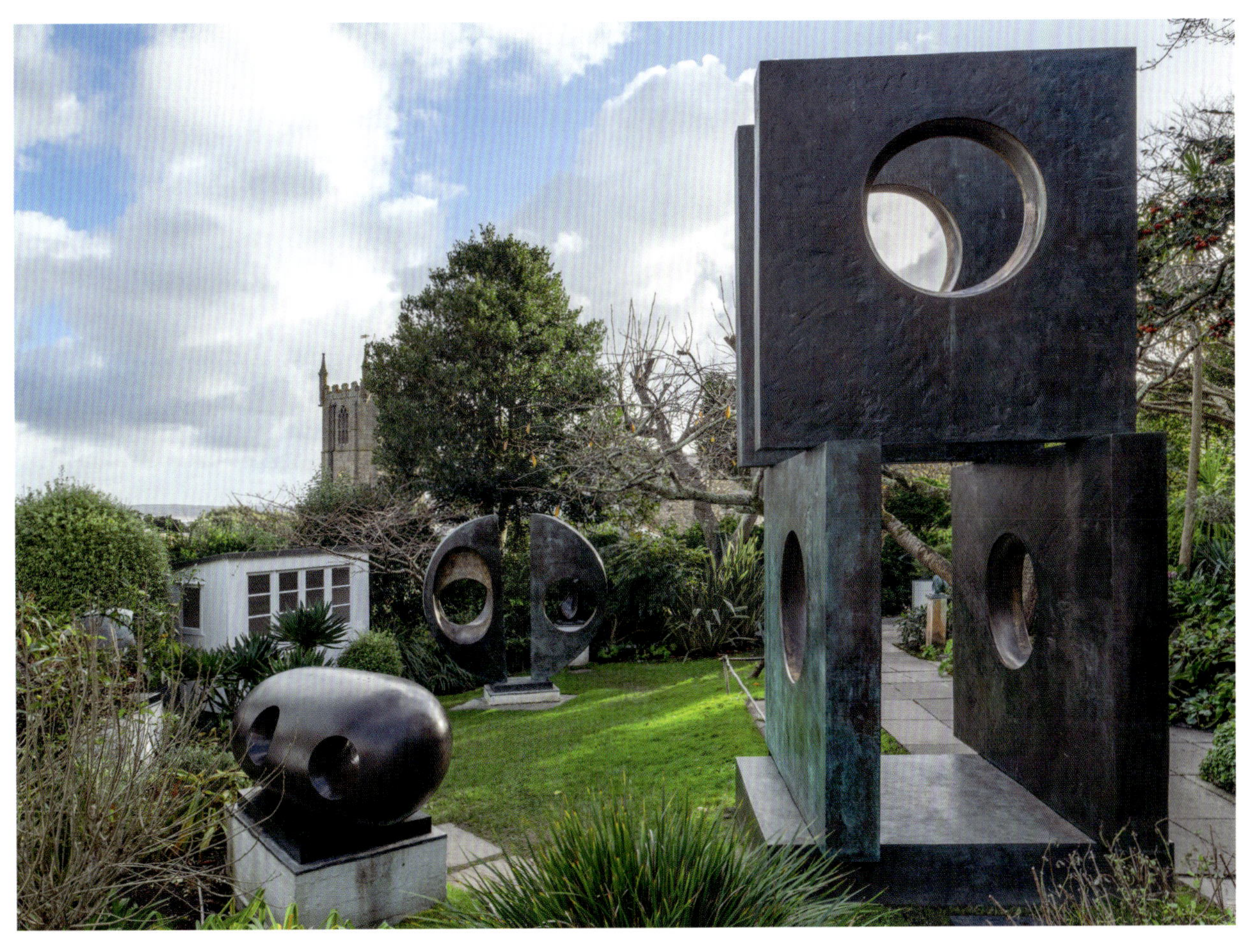

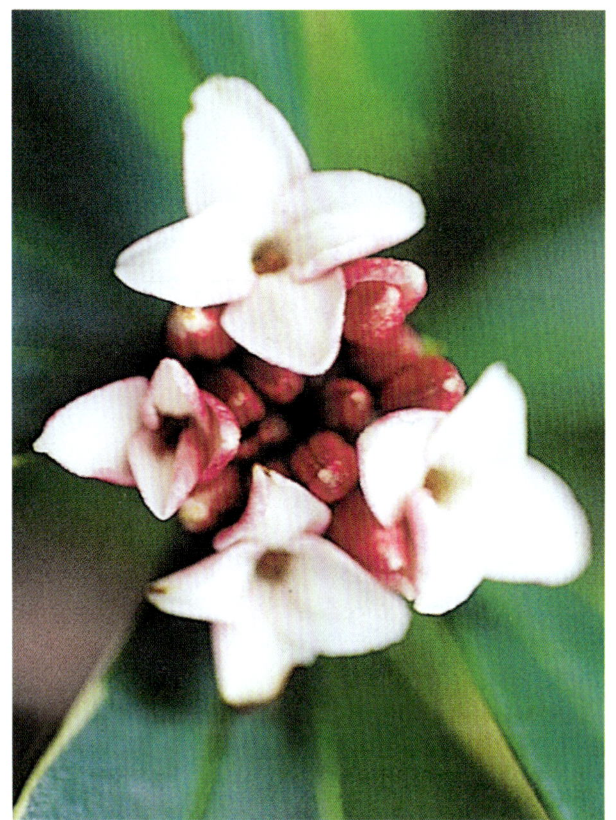

30 *Daphne odora* 'Aureomarginata' daphne

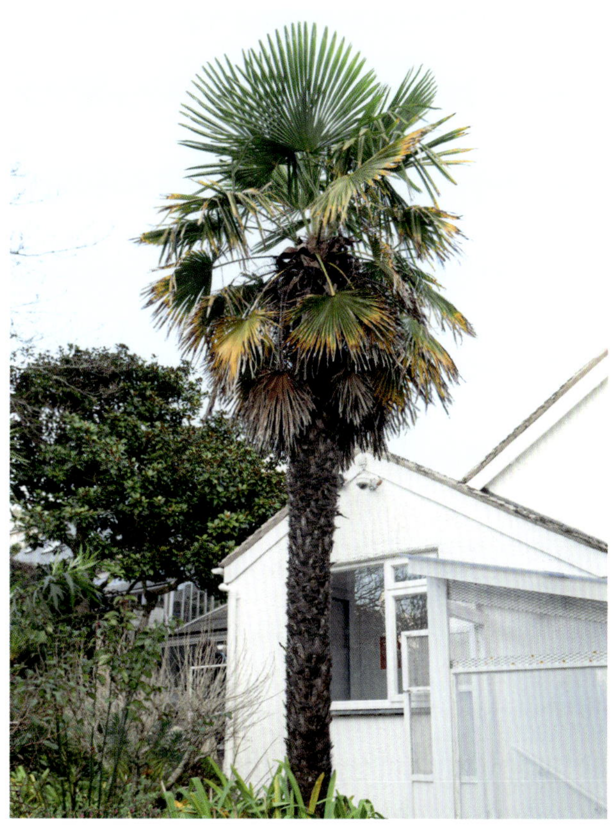

31 *Trachycarpus fortunei* Chusan palm

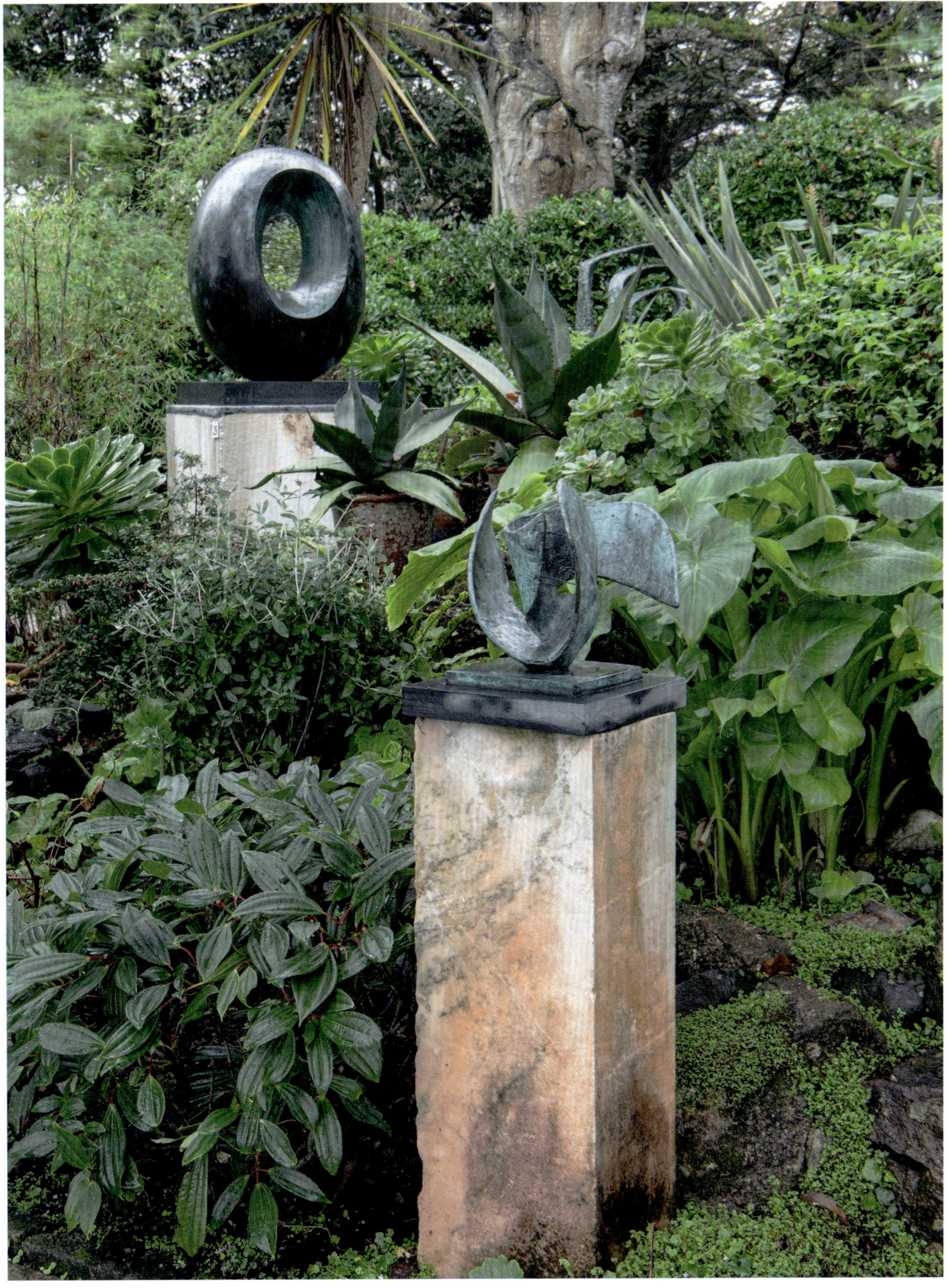

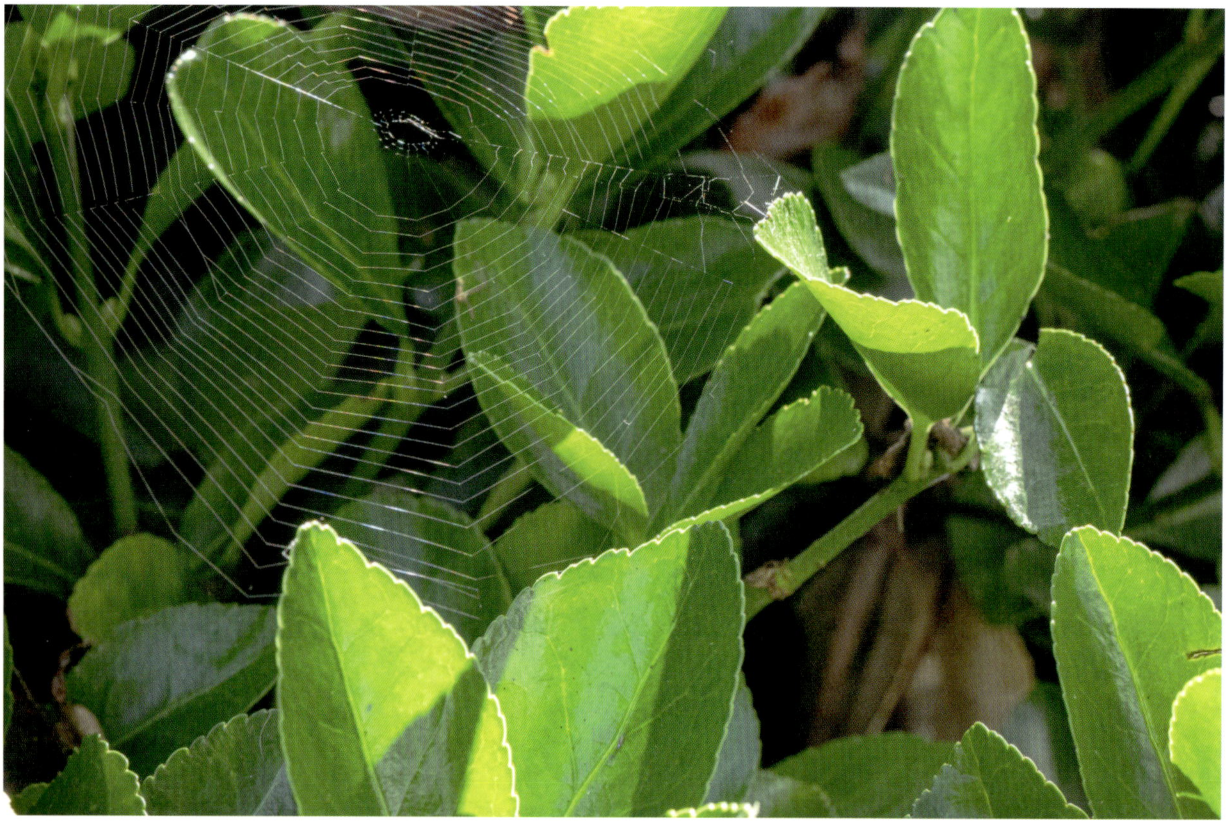

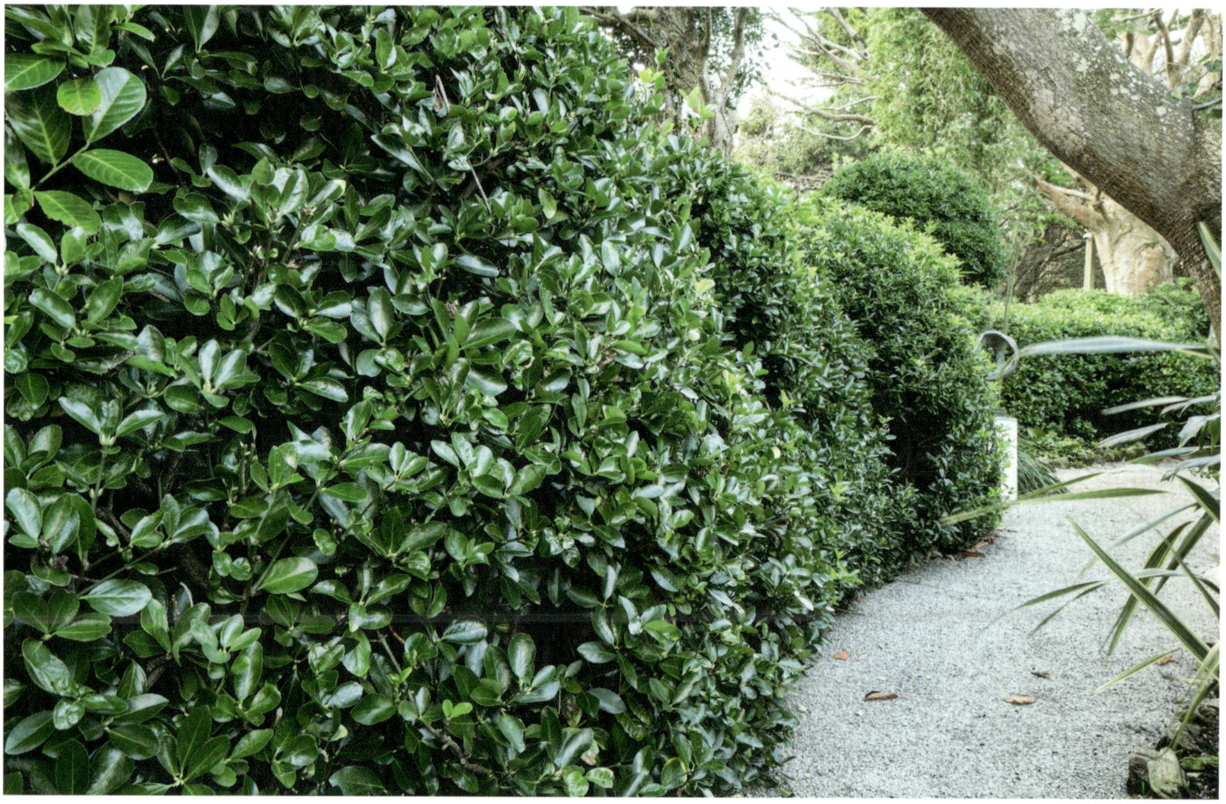

32 *Euonymus japonicus* Japanese spindle

30   *Daphne odora* 'Aureomarginata' daphne
Daphne odora is the most fragrant variety of a scented
genus. 'Aureomarginata' refers to the narrow, creamy
yellow margin around the glossy, dark green leaves. A
slow-growing evergreen, it forms a dense bushy shrub,
eventually reaching a height and spread of one and
a half metres. Small clusters of flowers start opening in
January and often continue into April. Each bloom is
a pale lilac-pink within and a deeper rose-purple on the
outside. Their perfume drifts across the garden in the
early spring and is heady, exotic and sweet – a couple
of sprigs in a glass will scent a room. Daphnes need
fertile, well-drained soil but must not be allowed to dry
out at the roots – a leaf-mould mulch will help avoid this.
All are frost hardy, some are fully hardy, and they all
need part to dappled shade to produce the finest
foliage and blossom.

31   *Trachycarpus fortunei* Chusan palm
Native to subtropical and temperate mountain forests
of China, the Chusan palm or Chinese windmill palm
was first introduced to Great Britain in 1849 by Robert
Fortune (1812–80). It has been cultivated in China and
Japan for thousands of years for making rope and
sacks where strength is of importance. Now however,
it is more widely cultivated for ornamental purposes,
providing a tropical touch to more temperate gardens
around the globe, as it is one of the cold-hardiest of
palms. Seeds can be spread by birds. The seedlings are
more temperature sensitive than mature plants; however,
given exposure to a mild winter, or a location close to
the sea, they can survive to become mature plants in
Cornwall. The Chusan palm has a solitary, fibre-covered
trunk that appears shaggy and hairy. The leaves are
dark green, fan-shaped and grow to one metre, or more
in shady areas. It is a delightful palm that grows in full
sun but does better in part shade with protection from
winds. There are three *Trachycarpus* in the museum
garden now; one is about twenty feet tall and growing
in full sun, the other two are more recently planted in
the woodland area to replicate some of the cordylines,
which have died off in the shade of the larger trees.

32   *Euonymus japonicus* Japanese spindle
An evergreen shrub or small tree native to Japan,
Korea and China, *Euonymus japonicus* can grow to eight
metres tall. It is a choice plant for hedging and wind
protection in Cornwall, being salt-tolerant, and will
create a beautiful, rich, dark green structure given
suitable growing conditions. The leaves have a thick,
glossy protective surface that keeps them looking
fresh and vibrant year-round. It grows well in the sun
and even better in shade and makes a superb foil to the
sculptures. It is used extensively at the museum garden;
the dark green is an important component to the calm
and contemplative atmosphere. Moreover, *Euonymus
japonicus*, along with holly, privet, olearia and griselinia

provide a crucial windbreak along the eastern
periphery, sheltering the garden from cold continental
winds. Relatively disease and problem free in Cornwall,
they can be shallow rooted so it is important to watch
for water stress, especially at the end of summer.

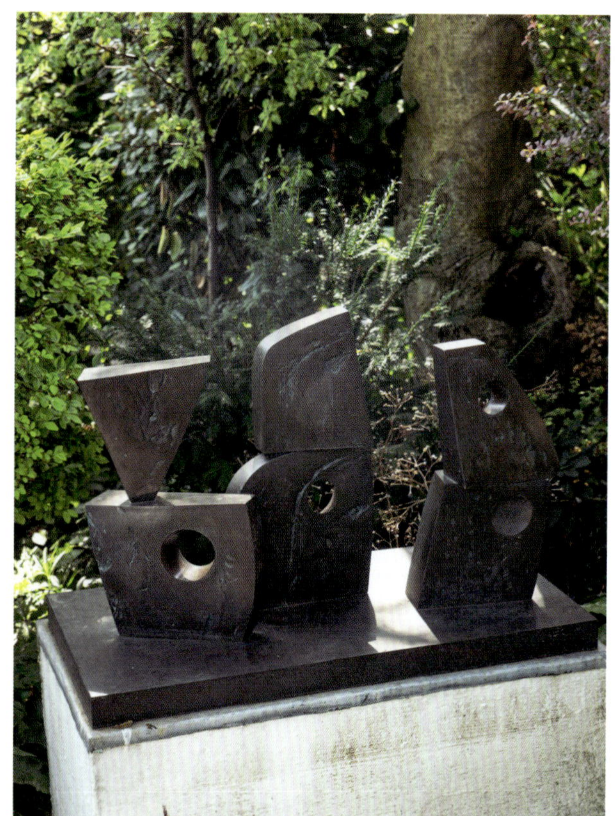

Six Forms (2 x 3) 1968

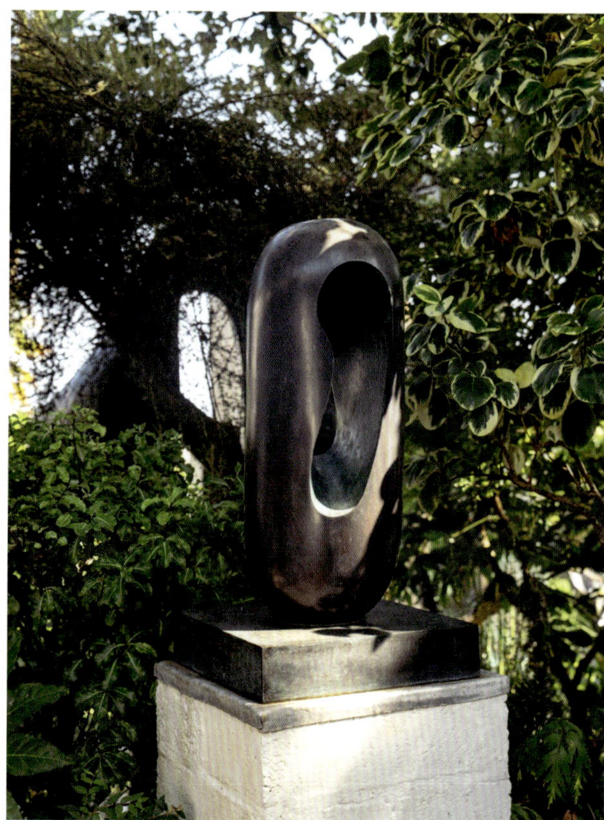

Makutu 1969, cast 1970

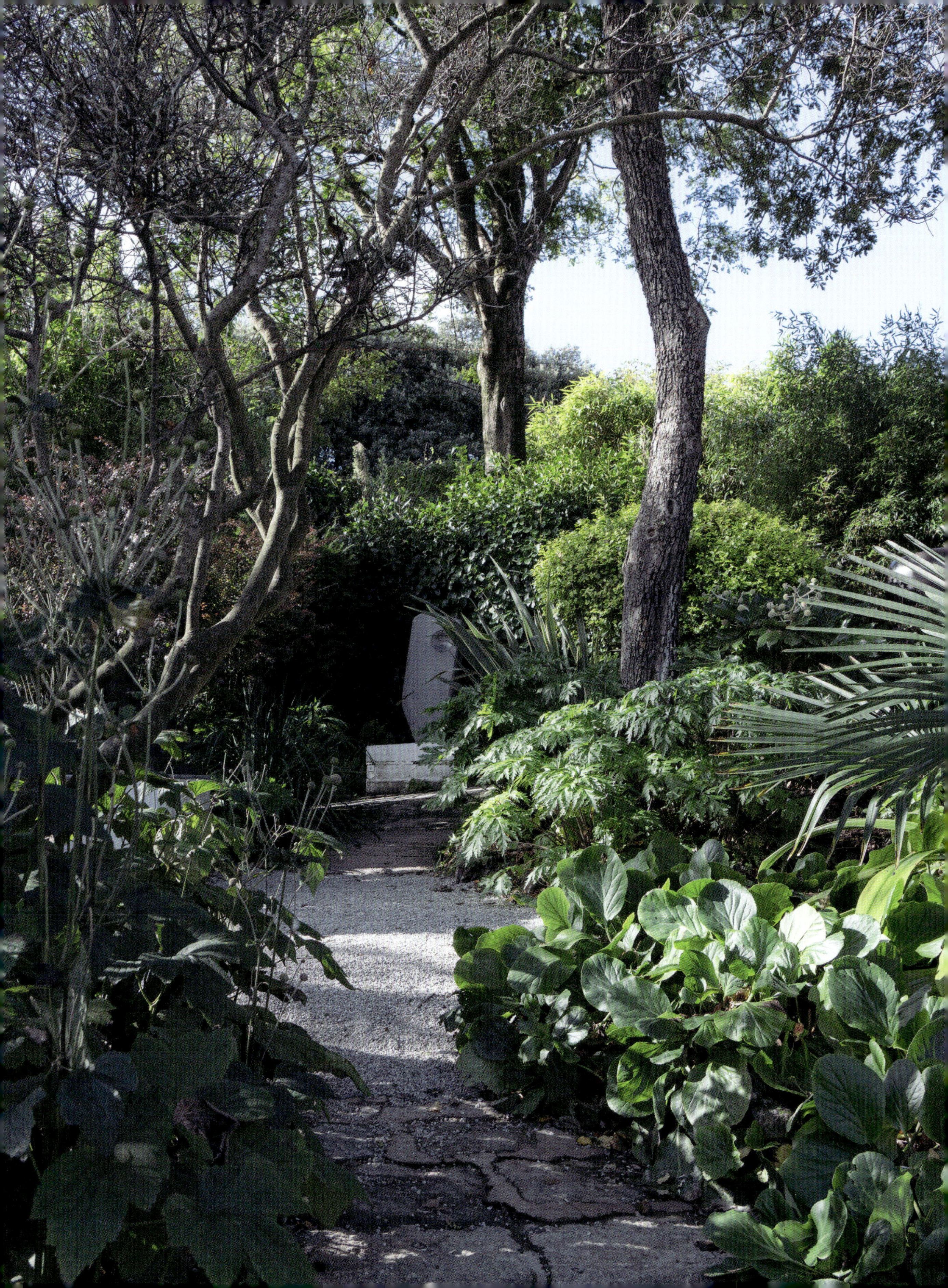

Chronology

1903   Born 10 January in Wakefield, Yorkshire,
        the eldest of four children.

1920–4 Studies sculpture at Leeds School of Art
        and Royal College of Art, London

1924–6 Travels in Italy. Marries sculptor John Skeaping
        in May 1925 in Florence, and the two study
        in Rome under the master-carver Ardini.

1926   November – returns to Britain and settles
        in St John's Wood, London.

1928   Moves to Mall studios, Hampstead,
        where she remains until 1939.

        June – first solo exhibition.

1929   Birth of a son, Paul.

1931   Meets the painter Ben Nicholson;
        they marry in 1938.

1932   Joint exhibition with Nicholson

1933   Easter – Hepworth and Nicholson travel
        to Provence via Paris; they are invited to join
        the avant-garde group *Abstraction-Création*.
        Hepworth and Skeaping divorce.

        June – the founding of *Unit 1* secures Hepworth
        and Nicholson a place at the heart of a British
        avant-garde.

1934   October – birth of triplets.

1939   August – the family move to Carbis Bay,
        St Ives, Cornwall. Conditions are not good
        and Hepworth makes few sculptures for
        several years.

1943   First retrospective exhibition,
        Temple Newsam, Leeds.

1946   First post-war solo exhibition,
        Alex. Reid & Lefevre, London.

1949   September – purchases Trewyn Studio

1950   Visits the Venice Biennale where she
        represents Britain.

1954   Major retrospective, Whitechapel Art Gallery,
        London. Visit to Greece inspires a group of
        large hardwood sculptures. Designs sets and
        costumes for composer Michael Tippett's
        Midsummer Marriage, Covent Garden, London.

1955–6 Major exhibition tours North America.

1958   Hepworth is created CBE; Nicholson leaves
        St Ives.

1959   Exhibition at São Paulo Biennal wins Grand
        Prix and tours South America.

1963   *Single Form* is commissioned for the United
        Nations, New York.

1964–5 Major exhibition tours Europe.

1965   Made Dame of the British Empire.

1966   Diagnosed with cancer of the throat; the
        disease is successfully treated.

1968   Retrospective, Tate Gallery, London.

1975   Having continued to work despite increasing
        frailty, Hepworth dies in a studio fire on 20 May.

Notes

A Sort of Magic
Chris Stephens

1   *Barbara Hepworth: A Pictorial Autobiography*,
     London 1970, rev. ed. 1978, p.52
2   Ibid.
3   John Anderson, 'Barbara Hepworth's Garden',
     The Cornish Garden, no.34, March 1991, p.24
4   Brian Smith, letter to the author, 29 June 1998
5   Brian Smith recalls twenty-six works in the garden
     that are no longer there, but some of these were
     removed during Hepworth's lifetime
6   J.P. Hodin, 'Barbara Hepworth and the
     Mediterranean Spirit', *Marmo*, no.3,
     December 1964, p.59
7   Ibid.

Trewyn Studio: Barbara Hepworth's Garden in St Ives
Miranda Phillips

1   Sarah Jane Checkland, *Ben Nicholson*, London 2000.
2   Trewyn House (then known as Halse's Court) was
     built by James Halse, solicitor, mine adventurer and
     Member of Parliament for St Ives. He also built the
     village of Halsetown, close to St Ives, to house his
     mineworkers and their families. 'Trewyn', a Cornish
     word, translates as 'the fair place' or 'the place
     of innocence'.
3   Now Trewyn Public Gardens. Both Hepworth and
     John Milne later donated plants for this garden.
4   W.H. Lane and Son, auction notice, September
     1949. The description recognises that suitable
     premises were saleable to artists. The garden is
     behind the Studio and greenhouse, not in front.
5   *Barbara Hepworth*, exh. cat., Marlborough-Gerson
     Gallery, New York 1966.
6   Sophie Bowness, *Barbara Hepworth: The Sculptor
     in the Studio*, p,54.
7   Ibid., p.39.
8   Ibid., p.77.
9   Will Arnold-Forster, *Shrubs for the Milder Counties*,
     London 1948, reprinted Penzance 2000.
     Hepworth's copy is now in the Tate Archive along
     with all of Hepworth's books.
10   Letter to Rainier, 27 November 1955.
11   John Milne was a former assistant of Hepworth's,
     later a sculptor in his own right. Trewyn House was
     bought for Milne by his patron, Professor Cosmo
     Rodewald in 1956 and Milne lived there until his
     death in June 1978.
12   Rainier purchased a small property in St
     Ives–Tregenna Steps Studio–in the early 1960s,
     dividing her time between St Ives and London,
     where she taught at the Royal Academy of Music.
     June Opie's book *'Come and listen to the Stars
     Singing'; Priaulx Rainier – A Pictorial Biography*,
     Penzance 1988, cites excerpts from Rainier's
     garden diary such as notes of flowering dates and
     bird and wildlife observations.
13   All copies of Hepworth's letters and legal
     documents quoted here are from the St Ives
     Archive.
14   Sophie Bowness, *The Sculptor in the Studio*, p.79
15   The majority of the cacti in the greenhouse
     belonged to one of Hepworth's assistants, Norman
     Stocker. When moving house he had nowhere to
     keep them; Hepworth offered to look after them
     temporarily, but they were never collected. As she
     already owned several these new additions were
     much enjoyed.
16   The Freedom of St Ives was awarded for Hepworth's
     contribution to the town in civic, as well as artistic,
     terms: she was an active member of the St Ives
     Trust, which acted to preserve St Ives' historic and
     architectural heritage; she had been a founder
     member of Cornwall County Council's 'Art in Schools'
     programme, and hadt given sculptures to the town.
     Hepworth's bardic name was 'Gravyor' (Sculptor).
17   M. Williams, newspaper article, 1988.
18   St Ives Times, 1976 and 1977.
19   Hepworth kept up to four cats at any one time
     while she lived at Trewyn Studio–they appear in
     many of the archive photographs. She fitted all of
     them with collars and bells, but it is unlikely that
     this deterred them from hunting.

Further Reading

A.M. Hammacher, Barbara Hepworth, London 1968,
rev. ed. 1987
Barbara Hepworth: A Pictorial Autobiography,
London 1970, rev. ed. 1978
Sally Festing, Barbara Hepworth: A Life of Forms,
Harmondsworth 1995
David Thistlewood (ed.), Barbara Hepworth
Reconsidered, Liverpool 1996
Penelope Curtis, St Ives Artists: Barbara Hepworth,
London 1998
Matthew Gale and Chris Stephens, Barbara Hepworth:
Works in the Tate Collection and the Barbara Hepworth
Museum St Ives, London 1999
Sophie Bowness, Barbara Hepworth: Writings and
Conversations, London 2015
Sophie Bowness, Barbara Hepworth: The Sculptor in
the Studio, London 2017

First published 2002, this revised edition published 2022 by order of the Tate Trustees by Tate Publishing, a division of Tate Enterprises Ltd, Millbank, London SW1P 4RG
www.tate.org.uk

© Tate Enterprises 2022

Reprinted 2025

Works and writings by Barabara Hepworth © Bowness

Information on plants by Jodi Dickinson with Miranda Phillips and captions on Hepworth's sculpture kindly provided by Chris Stephens.

All rights reserved. No part of this book may be reprinted or reproduced or utilised in any form or by any electronic, mechanical or other means, now known or hereafter invented, including photocopying and recording, or in any information storage or retrieval system, without permission in writing from the publishers or a licence from the Copyright Licensing Agency Ltd, www.cla.co.uk

The moral rights of the authors have been asserted
A catalogue record for this book is available from the British Library

ISBN 978-1-84976-794-1

Distributed in the United States and Canada by ABRAMS, New York Library of Congress Control Number applied for

Please note this book will not always accurately reflect the sculptures and plants in the Barbara Hepworth Sculpture Garden as changes are made. For more information see: www.tate.org.uk

Editor: Emilia Will
Production: Roanne Marner
Design: Sarah Krebietke
Colour reproduction by Altaimage, London
Printed and bound in Italy by Printer Trento S.r.l.
Measurements of artworks are given in centimetres, height before width and depth

Frontispiece:
Barbara Hepworth in Trewyn Studio garden, 15 May 1970, Studio St Ives © Bowness

Acknowledgements for original edition:
John Anderson, Bob Berry, Sir Alan Bowness, Brian Smith. Thanks also to Peter B. Evans

Photographic credits
© Tate (Joe Humphrys) 20-21, 77, 84, 87
© Tate (Oli Cowling) 4, 61, 62, 66, 67, 79, 82, 86, 93
© Tate (Matt Greenwood) 23, 25, 74, 89
© Tate (Matt Greenwood and Seraphina Neville) 27, 30, 35, 36, 38, 41, 46 (above), 64, 71 (below), 78 (left), 81 (left)
© Tate (Sonal Bakrania) 81 (right), 88, 90 (below)
© Tate (Bob Berry) 46 (below), 47, 88 (left)
© Kirstin Prisk 24, 31, 32, 34, 39–40, 43–5, 49–50, 51 (left), 52–9, 63–5, 68–9, 71 (above), 72–3, 78 (right), 80, 90, (above), 92, front cover (left), right flap (above), left flap (below), back cover (above, below)
© Jodi Dickinson 26, 28, 51 (right), front cover (above, right)
© Bowness 6, 10, cover (below, right)
Tate Gallery Archive, photo: Crispin Eurich 17
Studio St Ives © Bowness 2, 11, 12, 16, 19, left flap (above), right flap (below)
Official Festival of Britain Photograph 9

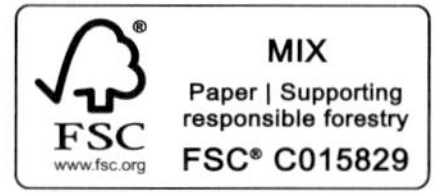